Business Skills in Physical Therapy:
Defining Your Business

Laurita Hack, PT, PhD, MBA, FAPTA

Laurita M Hack received her MS in physical therapy from Case Western Reserve University, her MBA from the Wharton School of the University of Pennsylvania, and her PhD in higher education administration from the University of Pennsylvania. She was an owner and the manager of a large physical therapy practice and is currently chair of Temple University's program in physical therapy. In addition to these 'real world' management activities, she has taught these principles of planning to hundreds of physical therapy students and practitioners. Her favorite planning activity is working with her colleagues to create big, hairy, audacious goals and then get them implemented.

Richard W Hillyer, PT, MBA, MSM

Richard W Hillyer, PT, MBA, MSM, has worked as the corporate human resources officer in a large contract rehab management company, as a self-employed owner of a multi-site physical therapy rehab agency, and as a rehabilitation services director in a large integrated health system. He has taught graduate economics, finance and accounting, and decision science for an eastern business school, and rehabilitation administration, leadership, entrepreneurship, and legal and ethical issues in health care for a state university's graduate health sciences programs. He has lectured nationally to professional groups on economic and business issues in rehabilitation practice.

Peter R Kovacek, PT, MSA

Author and Business Skills Series Editor Peter R Kovacek, PT, MSA, is president and chief executive officer of Kovacek Management Services Inc and In Home Rehab LLC, Harper Woods, Michigan, and co-owner of 1st Choice Physical Therapy LLC, Sterling Heights, Michigan. A widely known author, lecturer, and consultant, he is past president of the APTA Section on Administration (1999-2002) and a long-time member of the Acute Care/ Hospital Clinical Practice, Education, and Private Practice sections. He received a BS in Physical Therapy from Marquette University and a master's degree in Administration from Central Michigan University.

Business Skills in Physical Therapy: Defining Your Business

ISBN 978-1-931369-09-1

For more information about this and other publications, contact the American Physical Therapy Association, 1111 North Fairfax Street, Alexandria, VA 22314-1488; 800/999-2782, ext 3395; www.apta.org. [Publication No. BS-2]

Table of Contents

Preface

APTA's Business Skills Home-Study Series is designed to meet the needs of physical therapists who find themselves making business decisions related to their practice. Although the focus of the course series is to provide the fundamental skills and background knowledge in business management needed by all physical therapists who wish to function effectively in the current and future health care marketplace, it is also appropriate for experienced managers seeking an introductory business skills program.

This installment of the Business Skills Series is *Defining Your Business* by Laurita Hack, PT, PhD, MBA, FAPTA, Richard W Hillyer, PT, MBA, MSM, and Peter R Kovacek, PT, MSA. Drawing on the wisdom of such business gurus as Peter Drucker and Abraham Maslow, these experts have pulled together an overview of the various aspects of business that every physical therapist needs to consider, whether an entrepreneurial manager (business owner) or a manager working as an employee of a larger organization. Included in this home-study course are the following:

- Course objectives.

- Examination of the systems and structures used to organize businesses to effectively provide the services customers need.

- Guidance for developing and implementing a strategic plan.

- Discussion of different management systems and structures that have evolved in the context of contemporary business practices.

- Case studies illustrating the organizational and management concepts.

- A glossary of terms.

- Selected bibliographic references.

- A final examination to test the reader's understanding of key concepts.

Instructional Level: Basic to intermediate.

Audience: *Business Skills in Physical Therapy: Defining Your Business* is designed for physical therapists and physical therapist assistants. It also may be useful for physical therapy students as part of their studies toward a professional (entry-level) physical therapist education. (See note below about students and continuing education units.)

Continuing Education Units (CEUs): .6 CEUs, or 6 contact hours.

APTA does not impose time restrictions on the completion of this home-study course, so you may complete it at a pace that best suits your needs and learning style. You can work at your own pace, when it's convenient for you!

After reading this book, complete the final examination when you feel ready. Return the completed final examination answer sheet and the participant evaluation to APTA. Once you successfully complete the examination, a certificate of completion will be mailed to you in 3 to 4 weeks after receipt of your exam.

Special note to students who use this course: Please be advised that students pursuing a physical therapist professional education who acquire continuing education units (CEUs) through successful completion of the final exam cannot use these CEUs to fulfill physical therapist "relicensure" requirements. CEUs are applicable to *currently* licensed physical therapists meeting state board requirements for relicensure. In addition, CEUs are valid only during a specified licensing period and cannot be held for future use.

Best of luck as you proceed on your professional journey!

Peter Kovacek, PT, MSA
Business Skills Series Editor

Learning Objectives

Upon completion of this home-study course, the learner will be able to:

- Compare and contrast organizational theories and their application within the medical rehabilitation community.

- Compare and contrast theories that describe how organizations develop and behave.

- Define strategic planning.

- Recognize the similarities of strategic planning to other planning processes, including designing a patient's/client's plan of care.

- Describe the philosophy of strategic planning and its importance as a process for an organization's progress.

- Identify the key questions that must be answered to define one's business.

- Describe the process of developing a business's vision.

- List the steps in the complete planning process.

- Employ specific techniques for setting goals.

- Examine the fundamentals of supervision, including delegation, effective counseling, coaching, authority style, and providing direction.

- Recognize the most common reasons why today's organizations are involved in projects to restructure, reengineer, or reorganize their design systems.

- Identify the differences in various processes that organizations use to adapt to change.

Chapter 1

Introduction

This course in the Business Skills in Physical Therapy series will focus on organizational theory, strategic planning, and management theory. Although much of the material covered will be addressed from an academic perspective, an ample supply of physical therapy examples, vignettes, and case studies will help the reader apply these basic business concepts to real-world situations. Throughout this course, the material will cover two perspectives: that of the entrepreneurial manager (business owner) and that of the manager working as an employee of a larger organization. The intent in presenting these two perspectives is not to fragment the profession into divergent camps, but rather to highlight the differences in skill sets and strategies that may be needed by any physical therapy manager—whether owner or employee. This is especially important as the health care environment continues to change rapidly.

The course begins with an examination of the systems and structures used to organize businesses to effectively provide the services customers need. Systems and structures to consider in the development of physical therapy organizations will be reviewed in detail, and such concepts as motivation, quality of work life, performance enhancement, and job design will be addressed. This course also will examine the core documents of organizations: mission statements, vision statements, and strategic plans.

The second major component of this chapter focuses on management theory, with a focus on the various ways in which different management systems and structures have evolved in the context of contemporary business practices. This section will review the principles of management as they are applied to existing and evolving physical therapy business structures. It will explore the palette of management and leadership skills that physical therapists, including managers, must employ as they revolve through the many different roles required by today's dynamic health care environment.

Throughout, this course will explore the concept of organizational influence from the perspective of the manager of a physical therapy practice. It will examine key factors and concepts of developing influence both internal to a physical therapy practice and with external organizations.

At the conclusion of this course are two comprehensive case studies—one focusing on a private physical therapy clinic and one focusing on management of physical therapy services that are part of a larger organization.

Chapter 2

Business Organization

Organizational theory is the study and application of knowledge about how staff, individuals, and groups act in organizations. It does this by taking a *system approach*;[1] that is, it interprets people-organization relationships in terms of the whole person, whole group, whole organization, and whole social system. Its purpose is to build better relationships by achieving human objectives, organizational objectives, and social objectives. Organizational behavior encompasses a wide range of topics, such as human behavior, change leadership, teams, and so on.

Elements of Organizational Behavior

The organization's base rests on management's philosophy, values, vision, and goals. This in turn drives an organizational culture that is composed of the formal organization, informal organization, and the social environment. The culture determines the type of leadership, communication, and group dynamics within the organization.[2-5] The employees perceive this "culture" as the quality of work life that directs their degree of motivation. The final outcomes are performance, individual satisfaction, and personal growth and development. All these elements combine to build the model or framework from which the organization operates.

Models of Organizational Behavior

Organizational theory suggests that there are four major models or frameworks[6,7] within which organizations operate:

1. **Autocratic.** The basis of this model, which had its roots in the Industrial Revolution, is *power*, with a managerial orientation of *authority*. The employees are oriented toward obedience and dependence on the boss. The employee need that is met is subsistence. The performance result is minimal.

2. **Custodial.** The basis of this model is *economic resources*, with a managerial orientation of *money*. The employees are oriented toward security and benefits and dependence on the organization. The employee need that is met is security. The performance result is passive cooperation.

3. **Supportive.** The basis of this model is *leadership*, with a managerial orientation of *support*. The employees are oriented toward job performance and participation. The employee need that is met is status and recognition. The performance result is awakened drives.

4. **Collegial.** The basis of this model is *partnership*, with a managerial orientation of *teamwork*. The employees are oriented toward responsible behavior and self-discipline. The employee need that is met is self-actualization. The performance result is moderate enthusiasm.

Each model has evolved over a period of time, and there is no one "best" model. The collegial model should not be thought of as the last or best model, but the beginning of a new model or paradigm. Also, although there are four distinct models, virtually no organization operates exclusively within one style. Typically one model predominates within an organization and one or more other models overlap with it.

Table 1 illustrates a typical statement that might be made by a physical therapy manager based on each of these four models of organizational behavior in three situations:

- The decision by the manager to offer a job to a candidate

- The disciplinary counseling session that occurs when performance is not as desired

- The performance planning session

Organizational Development

Organizational development (OD) is the systematic application of behavioral science knowledge at various levels, such as group, inter-group, and organization-wide, to bring about planned change. OD is a field of applied behavioral science that focuses on understanding and managing

	Autocratic Style	Custodial Style	Supportive Style	Collegial Style
Hiring Decision	I have decided to hire you. You are fortunate to be able to work here.	We will pay you a good wage with excellent benefits if you accept this job.	I am pleased to be able to offer you this job. I think we can help you meet your career goals while you help us reach our organizational objectives.	I am looking forward to working with you. Together, there is so much that we can accomplish.
Disciplinary Action	You have not acted properly and I will now punish you.	It is important that you understand that your past performance is not acceptable so that you can learn for the future.	Once you can turn around this one problem area, you will be a significant asset to our work environment.	We can overcome this bump in the road—all we need to do is redouble our collective efforts to succeed.
Professional Development Planning	I've decided that you should pursue clinical specialization in orthopedics.	In the long run, you will be more valuable to us and to yourself if you pursue clinical specialization in orthopedics.	After you finish your specialization, you will be a great senior therapist who can help the junior staff and enhance your reputation—even outside this organization. Does that sound like something you'd find worth pursuing?	Your professional development is important. What can I do as your manager to help you accomplish your personal and professional goals?

Table 1. *Organizational Behavioral Models in Physical Therapy.*

organizational change.[7] OD relies on a collection of techniques that have a certain philosophy and body of knowledge in common. Its objectives are a higher quality of work-life, productivity, adaptability, and effectiveness. It accomplishes this by changing attitudes, behaviors, values, strategies, procedures, and structures so that the organization can adapt to competitive actions, technological advances, and the fast pace of *change* within the environment.

Organizational development is a basic responsibility of every manager. It is what allows a practice to be sustainable and to evolve over time.

There are seven characteristics of OD[3]:

1. **Humanistic Values.** There are positive beliefs about the potential of employees.

2. **Systems Orientation.** All parts of the organization, including structure, technology, and staff, work together.

3. **Experiential Learning.** The learners' experiences in the training environment are the kind of human problems they encounter at work. The training is not all theory and lecture.

4. **Problem Solving.** Problems are identified, data are gathered, corrective action is taken, progress is assessed, and adjustments in problem-solving processes are made as needed.

5. **Contingency Orientation.** Actions are selected and adapted to fit the need.

6. **Change Agent.** The process stimulates, facilitates, and coordinates change.

7. **Levels of Interventions.** Problems can occur at one or more levels in the organization, and thus the strategy will require one or more interventions.

Organizational Social Systems and Culture: Impact on Individualization

A social system is a complex set of human relationships interacting in many ways. Within an organization, the social system includes all the people in it and their relationships to each other and to the outside world. The behavior of one member can have an impact, either directly or indirectly, on the behavior of others. The social system does not have boundaries. It exchanges goods, ideas, and culture with the environment around it.

Culture is the conventional behavior of a society that encompasses beliefs, customs, knowledge, and practices.[8] It influences human behavior, even though it seldom enters into conscious thought. People depend on culture as it gives them stability, security, understanding, and the ability to respond to a given situation. This is why people fear change. They fear the system will become unstable, their security will be lost, they will not understand the new process, and they will not know how to respond to the new situations.

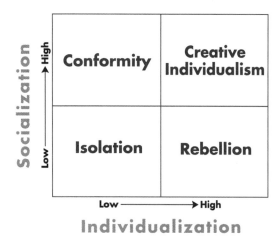

Figure. *The impact of individualization on an organization.*

Individualization occurs when employees successfully exert influence on the social system by challenging the culture.

The Figure illustrates how individualization affects different organizations:

- Too little socialization and too little individualization create isolation.

- Too much socialization and too little individualization create conformity.

- Too little socialization and too high individualization create rebellion.

Organizations want to create high socialization and high individualization for a creative environment. This is what it takes to survive in a very competitive environment.

This can become quite a balancing act. Individualism favors individual rights, loosely knit social networks, self-respect, and personal rewards and careers. Socialization or collectivism favors the group, harmony, and asks, "What is best for the organization?" Organizations are most likely to thrive when staff challenge, question, and experiment while maintaining the culture that binds them into a social system.[4,9,10]

The Challenge of Diversity in Organizations

One of the great challenges facing many organizations is getting *all* employees, from the CEO to the hourly employees, to realize that to become the best, they have to embrace diversity. Every team-building theory states that to build a great team, there must be a diverse group of staff on the team; that is, you must avoid choosing only staff who are like you.

Why Should Physical Therapy Managers Embrace Diversity?

Diversity is about empowering people. It makes an organization effective by capitalizing on all of the strengths of each employee. It is not Equal Employment Opportunity or Affirmative Action; these are laws and policies, and simply enforcing government regulations will not allow an organization to rise to its greatest potential. Diversity is understanding, valuing, and using the differences in every person to fulfill the organization's mission.

If team members do not accept others for who they are, they will not be able to use the abilities of others to fill in their weak areas, and the team effort will fail. Their goal becomes whatever serves their personal agendas, often to make the individual look good while ignoring the needs of the team. By engaging all staff to embrace diversity, team effort will benefit, as will the organization's ability to reach or exceed its mission. The essence of diversity should NOT be to picture diversity as race, religion, sex, and age; but to picture it as *every individual is unique*. Only by accepting the uniqueness of others will staff want to help the team as a whole to succeed.

Why Is Embracing Diversity a Challenge?

Biases and prejudices are deeply rooted within individuals. From the moment a person is born, he or she begins to learn about the environment, the world, and his or herself. Family, friends, peers, teachers, idols, books, and other influences "teach" that person what is right and what is wrong. These early learnings shape a person's perceptions about how we view things and how we respond to them. What we learn and experience gives us our *subjective point of view,* known as bias. Our biases serve as filters that allow us to make sense of new information and experiences based on what we already know. Many of our biases are good, as they allow us to assume that something is true without proof. (Otherwise, we would have to start learning anew on everything that we do.) But if we allow our biases to shade our perceptions of, for example, what staff members are capable of, then the biases become harmful. We may fall in the trap of prejudging others based on what we think they can and cannot do.

Simply attending a class on diversity will not erase these biases. Indeed, even the best training will not disrupt most of these deeply rooted beliefs. Training can only help us to become aware of them so that we can make a conscious effort to change. Diversity training is more than a two-hour class; it involves workshops, role models, one-on-ones, and other techniques. But most of all, it involves a heavy commitment by the organization's leadership, both the formal leadership and the informal leadership that can be found in almost every organization.

Embracing diversity is more than tolerating people who are different. It means actively welcoming and involving them by:

- Developing an atmosphere in which it is safe for all employees to ask for help. Staff should not be viewed as weak if they ask for help. This is what helps to build great teams - joining weaknesses with strengths to get the goal accomplished.

- Actively seeking information from people from a variety of backgrounds and cultures, and including everyone in the problem-solving and decision-making process.

Why Does Diversity Matter?

Organizations have begun to realize that all cultures of the world are their potential customers. Not too long ago, many businesses focused on the young and/or middle-aged white customer. This was where the money was. Now, thanks to great efforts toward recognizing the many facets of diversity and the good that it brings us, money is in the hands of people from a wide range of cultural backgrounds. But in order to attract this wide variety of cultures to their customer base, organizations must truly become multi-cultural themselves. People of other cultures will not tolerate organizations that employ only "people of their kind" in leadership and high-visibility positions. These cultures will spend their money with organizations that truly believe in diversity. Embracing diversity has several benefits for the organization:

- It is the right moral thing to do. To attract good staff into their ranks, organizations must take the moral path.

- It allows the organization to attract staff from the entire population rather than just a segment of the population.

- It helps to build teams that create synergy...you get more for your efforts.

- It broadens their customer base in a very competitive environment.

■ Including people who are different than you in informal gatherings, such as lunch, coffee breaks, and spur-of-the-moment meetings.

■ Creating a team spirit in which every member feels a part of the team.

What Exactly Does Diversity Include?

Most organizations picture diversity in very limited terms. Diversity goes beyond black and white, female and male, gay and heterosexual, Jew and Christian, young and old. It also includes slow learner and fast learner, introvert and extrovert, "controlling" type and "people" type, scholar and sports-person, liberal and conservative, and so on. It should be every manager's priority to help staff realize that it takes a wide variety of people to form an effective team and that each individual should be able to rely on everyone on their team, no matter how different another person may be. An organization *needs* controllers, thinkers, dreamers, doers, organizers, team builders, and others to reach the goals that make an organization the best it can be.

References

1. Hampton DR, Summer CE, Webber RA. *Organizational Behavior and the Practice of Management, 4th Ed.* Glenview, Ill: Scott, Foresman and Co; 1982.

2. Montana PJ, Charnow BH. *Management, 2nd Ed.* Haupauge, NY: Barrons; 1993.

3. Hodge BJ, Anthony WP. *Organization Theory, 2nd Ed.* Boston, Mass: Allyn and Bacon Inc; 1984.

4. Hersey P, Blanchard KH, Johnson DE. *Management of Organizational Behavior—Utilizing Human Resources, 7th Ed.* Upsaddle River, NJ: Prentice Hall; 1996.

5. Walter J. *Physical Therapy—An Integrated Science.* St Louis, Mo: Mosby; 1993.

6. Nosse LJ, Friberg DG, Kovacek PR. *Managerial and Supervisory Principles for Physical Therapists.* Baltimore, MD: Lippincott Williams and Wilkins; 1998.

7. Cooper CL, Argyris C. *The Concise Blackwell Encyclopedia of Management.* Malden, Mass: Blackwell Publishers; 1998.

8. Schwartz SH, Sagiv L. Identifying culture-specifics in the content and structure of values. *Journal of Cross-cultural Psychology.* 1995;26.

9. Boone LE, Kurtz DL. *Contemporary Business, 7th Ed.* New York, NY: Dryden Press; 1993.

10. Dilenschneider RL. *Power and Influence: Mastering the Art of Persuasion.* New York, NY: Prentice Hall; 1990.

Chapter 3

Planning For Your Organization's Success

Introduction to Strategic Planning

The past three decades have produced an incredible amount of turbulence for the profession of physical therapy. Whether experiencing growth or constriction, *change* has become the byword. By all indications, change will continue, and at an unprecedented rate. This part of the Business Skills home study course will consider one of the primary means that physical therapists have to help manage this change—strategic planning.

Today, strategic planning is often offered as the solution to many problems—to build employee commitment, to rescue a failing unit or company, to demonstrate that an organization knows what it's doing, or to meet the requirements of an external regulating agency. These goals may well be achieved (sometimes!) by strategic planning, but its primary function is often overlooked. Strategic planning, according to Peter Drucker[1] is "the *continuous* process of making *entrepreneurial* (risk-taking) decisions *systematically* and with the greatest knowledge of their *futurity*; organizing systematically the efforts needed to carry out these decisions; and *measuring the result*s of these decisions against the expectations through organized, systematic feedback."[1]

There are several important features in Drucker's definition.

Continuous. All too often a strategic plan is created by a small group of people and then put on the shelf to be presented to various reviewers as evidence that the group has engaged in planning. But this type of plan, even if it is 100 pages long and took months to complete, is not strategic planning. Instead strategic planning must be ongoing and ever changing in response to changes in the environment—just like evaluation and planning with patients.

Entrepreneurial. Drucker returns to the origins of this word, which too often has come to mean looking out for oneself. Instead, entrepreneurial means choosing to take risks to make gains. Physical therapists often deny that they are entrepreneurs or are even interested in entrepreneurial ideas. What they usually mean is that they are not very interested in business aspects of practice or they don't want anyone to think that they place monetary concerns before the needs of the patient/client. But doesn't Drucker's definition—the willingness to take risk in the face of uncertainty to make gains—sound a lot like what physical therapists do each day as they work with patients/clients? In fact, recent research has demonstrated that one of the characteristics of master clinicians is this willingness to take risks with patients/clients to achieve the best outcomes.[2]

Systematically. Strategic planning needs to occur in an organized fashion. There are many systems put forward to do strategic planning. All of them have in common that planners must understand their own basic values, scan the environment, and have knowledge of the resources and constraints that currently exist. Planners then use this information to develop anticipated goals or expected outcomes and identify the resources and actions required to meet the goals within a specific time frame. Again, this process should sound very familiar to clinicians—it is exactly the process used in patient/client management—examination and evaluation, diagnosis, prognosis, and designing a plan of care for that patient/client.

Futurity. Understanding and predicting the future may indeed be the most difficult part of strategic planning. The future is *never* completely known. Instead managers must rely on probabilities to help them in planning. Estimating risk and probability is one of the most difficult types of decision-making in which human beings engage.[3] It is the difficulty in this estimation that produces the risk in planning. Luckily, much work has been done to identify common biases in decision-making and the heuristics, or decision rules, that can be used to overcome these biases.[4] But once again, it is useful to remember that physical therapists face this same need to predict the future each time they determine a prognosis for a patient.

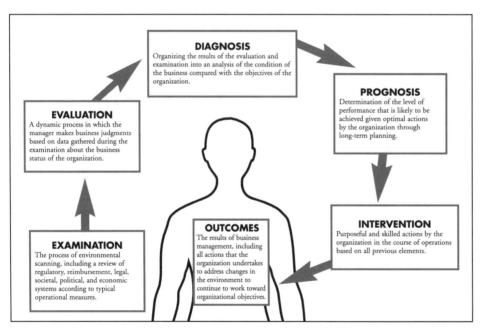

Measuring the results. A strategic plan must go full circle by including measures to determine if the expected outcomes have been met. The final step of the plan, then, is to implement these measures to assess the level of success in meeting the expected outcomes. Once more, strategic planning mirrors what physical therapists do each time they assess patients/clients for possible discharge.

Figure 1. *The elements of business management leading to optimal outcomes. (Adapted from the Guide to Physical Therapist Practice, 2nd Ed, Phys Ther, 2001;81:9-744, with permission of the American Physical Therapy Association.)*

These features have been selected because they represent the essence of strategic planning. They also reflect the universality of the process of planning. Whether a physical therapist is engaged in planning with a specific patient/client for his or her care, carrying out a quality improvement activity, participating in a clinical research project, or doing strategic planning, the same logical process holds. The activities of APTA's former Section on Administration (merged with the Section on Health Policy, Legislation, and Regulation in 2002 to form the Section on Health Policy and Administration) to create the Leadership, Administration, Management, and Professionalism (LAMP) project[5] demonstrate very clearly the relationship of the patient/client care process to the management process. As Figure 1 demonstrates, the patient/client management model presented in the *Guide to Physical Therapist Practice*[6] easily can be adapted to be a model of management processes.

The Table provides further comparison of the elements of business management to the elements of clinical management.

Five Initial Questions

One of the most read authors in management is Peter Drucker. In his classic text, *Management: Tasks, Responsibilities, Practice,* Drucker emphasizes the importance of strategic planning as one of the most important tasks of a manager.[1] Once managers recognize that all business decisions require taking risk, they can see why Drucker places strategic planning at the heart of management decision making.

Drucker also says that the first, and perhaps most important, step to minimize risk is to have

Element	Clinical Management Description[5]	Business Management Description[6]
Examination	The process of obtaining a history, performing relevant systems reviews, and selecting and administering specific tests and measures to obtain data.	The process of environmental scanning, including systems review of: regulatory, reimbursement, legal, societal, political, and economic systems according to typical operational measures.
Evaluation	A dynamic process in which the physical therapist makes clinical judgments based on data gathered during the examination.	A dynamic process in which the manager makes business judgments based on data gathered during examination of the business status of the organization.
Diagnosis	Both the process and the end result of evaluating information obtained from the examination, which the physical therapist then organizes into defined clusters, syndromes, or categories to help determine the most appropriate intervention strategies.	Organizing the results of the evaluation and examination into an analysis of the condition of the business compared with the objectives of the organization.
Prognosis	Determination of the level of optimal improvement that might be attained through intervention and the amount of time required to reach that level.	Determination of the level of performance that is likely to be achieved given optimal actions by the organization based on long-term planning.
Intervention	Purposeful and skilled interaction of the physical therapist with the patient/client and, if appropriate, with other individuals involved in the care of the patient/client, using various physical therapy methods and techniques to produce changes in the condition that are consistent with the diagnosis and prognosis.	Purposeful, skilled actions employed by the organization during the course of operations, based on all previous elements of this model.
Outcomes	The results of patient/client management, which includes remediation of functional limitation and disability, optimization of patient/client satisfaction, and primary or secondary prevention.	The results of business management, which includes all actions that the organization undertakes to address changes in the environment to continue to work toward organizational objectives.

Table. *Comparing the Elements of Clinical and Business Management Leading to Optimal Outcomes.*

a very clear concept of one's business. He says that managers should be able to clearly answer the question, *"What is our business?"* It is simple to say that the business of physical therapy is patient/client care, and that is certainly true. Yet all physical therapists actually participate in many different kinds of businesses.

Drucker proposes several questions that a manager can ask to define his or her business more clearly.

"Who is the customer?" Drucker considers this the most critical question. Of course, patients and clients who receive a physical therapist's direct care are primary customers. But, managers need to ask, "Which patients or clients?" A few practices, in large tertiary care centers, may believe that they can and should serve all types of patients. However, in most practices, physical therapists do

not intend to be able to care for all types of patients. Instead they select a niche, where they believe they have the interest, expertise, or potential to succeed.

Direct patients/clients are not a physical therapist's only customers. Certainly, referring sources, payers, and managed care companies are customers, because they are a primary source of patients. There are other customers as well. For physical therapists working with children, families and teachers may be customers. If they work with patients injured at work, employers and union representatives may be customers.

And there are still other customers as well. For example, nursing staff can be among a physical therapist's customers, as they play such an important role in both access to patients and the follow-through on the skills that patients have learned. If a manager has any interest at all in employee satisfaction—key to a high retention rate and to successful recruiting—then staff must be considered customers. Certainly, administrators or employers are customers.

So, there are really many customers. One of the greatest dilemmas of strategic planning is choosing among these many customers, some of who may have competing values. The next section will discuss how to identify the values held by customers. The end of this course also will explore the ethical dilemmas that arise in selecting among customers.

"What is value to the customer?" This question is really asking "Why does your customer choose your service, instead of someone else's service?" In today's health care system the primary customer, the patient, often no longer has the choice of site of service if he or she is relying on insurance to cover health care expenses. This choice is limited in many ways. Managed care organizations may limit choice through panel requirements. Patients may choose their doctor or hospital and then be required to accept the physical therapy practice associated with the organization, if they want to maximize the available reimbursement. Certainly within practices, even patients/clients who self-pay often do not choose the specific physical therapist who will provide their care. In addition, patients/clients often choose other providers, such as chiropractors and personal trainers, instead of physical therapists.

Physicians were once considered to have primary control over patient choice. The growth of both direct access and managed care has significantly lessened the role of physicians as the gatekeepers to our services. However, they still are very important customers who have their own perspective on what is value in physical therapy, often related to a perception of successful outcomes, but also including concern over patient satisfaction, and other organizational concerns.

Much of patient choice is controlled, first, by decisions made by employers about health care plans and then in the health care plans in selecting the physical therapy practices available to the consumer. It is easy to say that payers and managed care organizations have only one value—cost, but this would not be completely accurate.

Even if patients don't choose their practice or their physical therapist, they always have the choice to cooperate with the physical therapist's plan of care. The issues of health belief models, patient compliance, and patient satisfaction are complex and beyond the scope of this course, but they are important in understanding individual patient choice and the values that customers have. Drucker ends his discussion on the issue of value to the customer by saying that it would be foolish to try to presume what is value to customers—they need to be asked! So one of the important steps in strategic planning is to conduct a needs assessment—research to determine what different populations need and what their unique or special interests may be.

"What will our business be?" This question, and its companion question, *"What should our business be?"* are at the heart of strategic planning. To answer these questions, it is essential to understand the external environment, to do what many people call an external scan. In most businesses, and certainly in health care, this usually means starting with an understanding of population dynamics. This calls for a demographic analysis, which involves gathering such information as population growth/decline rate, age range, sex, and income/educational level for populations in general as well as for the populations in the specific region. Because the health care system is dynamic, trend analyses also must be included to anticipate the future actions of payers and regulatory agencies and of other aspects of economic change. An analysis of the competition that provides, or wants to provide, services to this population also is needed, as is the organization's own ability to anticipate the unmet needs of customers, because responding to these unmet needs assures stability and fuels the growth of the practice. This often means seeking out data on a regional or national level, beyond the confines of a single practice. It may be necessary to use data that compare regional patterns of utilization. Epidemiological analyses can offer information about incidence and prevalence. By combining this with evidence on efficacy managers can identify unmet needs of local populations.

By evaluating the environment, the competition, and customers' unmet needs, managers can determine how external forces alone will affect what their organization become. This allows managers to understand what will happen if they make no changes or what they need to do, at the very least, for the business to stay the same. If an organization really wants to reduce risk, assure future viability, and encourage growth, however, managers also should determine what they *want* the business to become, or what they believe it should be. Strategic planning provides the tools to increase an organization's control over external forces and to use these forces to its own advantage.

"What new things do we need to do, and when?" The final question that Drucker poses turns the rather abstract ideas from the previous questions into specific reality. A plan must include the actions that need to be taken, along with a timeframe to accomplish them. The plan often also identifies the person(s) responsible for achieving the goals. Later on in this chapter is a discussion of some techniques for assuring that the plan is implemented as conceived.

If managers are not answering these questions as they develop, use, and revise a strategic plan, then they are not really doing strategic planning. It is important to address another concern that physical therapists often express when the discussion turns to business and business growth. All too often, physical therapists can be heard saying, "I am not a business person, I am a physical therapist," or "Physical therapy is about patients, it is not a business." Physical therapy is indeed about patient/client care. And if physical therapists want to be able to manage their patients and clients in the manner they believe to be best, and if they want to keep that opportunity in the future, they *must* closely examine their services, their customers, and their environment, and they must make sound decisions for the future. In other words, they need to engage in continuous strategic planning.

Hollow Square Game

There are several exercises that are available to help groups understand the importance of having both those who plan and those who implement work closely together. One such exercise is the Hollow Square Game, which shows quite vividly that planners, when they do not have responsibility for implementation, are often too abstract and forgetful of important details. In the game implementers and planners are separated. The implementers must |wait while the planners prepare instructions for a detailed task. Once the planners are ready, they provide a short period of instruction and then must be silent while the implementers attempt to follow the directions to achieve the task. The implementers, because they usually do not understand the basic plan, are frustrated and have difficulty accomplishing the intended goal within the expected time frame. Planners become frustrated watching their instructions be misunderstood. This is a very useful exercise to try with your staff before beginning a planning process. It gives a good understanding of why everyone needs to engage in the planning process if it is to be truly successful.[8]

One thing to consider is who actually formulates the plan. The answer to this question relies in part to the management strategy that a manager has chosen (See Chapters 4–6). Planning can derive from the executive, the person with the ultimate responsibility for the business; from managers, the people who have the job of making sure that services are provided; or from the actual service providers themselves. Drucker's answer is very clear, however. He believes that a top-down plan can never be as useful as one that involves all those who will need to implement it. This is not surprising given that Drucker is a strong proponent—in fact one of the developers—of those management strategies, based on Maslow's hierarchy,[7] that say that employees need to be fully engaged in their work in order to maximize both their satisfaction and their productivity.

The Planning Success Cycle

One final point from Drucker concerns the timing of planning. All too often managers turn to a strategic plan to save a failing enterprise. A sound plan can sometimes work to successfully manage a crisis. However, Drucker refers to waiting for a crisis to plan as "irresponsible management."[1] A business should always be in the strategic planning mode. This means that a business is always somewhere in the cycle of assessing values, scanning, setting goals, implementing goals, and assessing success as a prelude for the next cycle. This "success planning cycle" includes the following steps: vision, mission, objectives, tasks, timelines, and follow-up (Figure 3).

Defining Vision, Mission, and Shared Values

Most of the systems for strategic planning today state that a business should identify its vision and its mission as a prelude for defining specific long- and short-range objectives in a strategic plan. Whether the entity is new or old, growing or retrenching, attempting to earn a profit or attempting to simply provide services, it must identify the very basic values, principles, and aspirations that give it its reason for being. These values, principles, and aspirations comprise the **vision** and **mission** of the enterprise. All of the organization's acts may rightly be expected to be in support of that vision and mission.

For managers of a unit that is a part of a larger organization, it is important to frame the vision and mission of the unit in the context of the vision and mission of the parent organization. A conflicting vision may actually be an indication of real organizational problems that need to be resolved before progress can be made.

Figure 3. *The success planning cycle.*

Vision

A **vision** also should address an ideal; for example, what a department or practice would look like if it were perfect, or what the most efficient way to produce a product would look like, or how the business would still provide high-quality services if budgets were reduced by 10 percent. The concept implies a long-term perspective, and a vision should last for many years. A vision usually is expressed as a short, clear statement:

Sample vision statements:

> American Physical Therapy Association Section on Health Policy and Administration[9]
> *Section members serve as leaders in professional practice, practice management, and health policy.*
>
> American Physical Therapy Association[10]
> *Vision Sentence: By 2020, physical therapy will be provided by physical therapists who are doctors of physical therapy, recognized by consumers and other health care professionals as practitioners of choice to whom consumers have direct access for the diagnosis of, interventions for, and prevention of impairments, functional limitations, and disabilities related to movement, function, and health.*
>
> Typical Physical Therapy Practice
> *XYZ Physical Therapy Practice will be seen as the best source of high quality outpatient care for people with neurological problems in our region.*
>
> Integrated Delivery System
> *ABC Health System will become the preferred source of comprehensive health care services in the tri-county area.*

This statement makes it clear what the business is, sets a standard for the business, and distinguishes it from competitors.

Because clarifying a business's vision is so important, it is worth spending a little more time on this step of the process. Collins and Porras[11] have done research on companies that are especially strong and enduring. They examined both product- and service-oriented industries in several countries. They identified that these companies all were "visionary companies." Visionary companies have two key characteristics: core ideology, made up of core values and core purpose; and an envisioned future. Collins and Porras are using the term vision differently from how it is commonly used in strategic planning. For them, vision is not simply a declarative statement, but

---

a way of doing business that places commonly held unifying values as the prime factor in all business decisions. Some businesses simply don't have core values and purposes that are commonly held by all key decision-makers. These businesses have much less chance of long-term success.

Collins and Porras describe core ideology as the glue that holds businesses together during times of turbulence. They recommend bringing together a group of key people—the ones with the most credibility with their peers, high levels of competence, and good ability to be reflective. The first step is to ask this group to identify their own personal values related to work. They recommend asking some very blue-sky types of questions, such as:

▪ Would you hold these values if you became suddenly very rich?

▪ Would you share these values with your children?

▪ Do you think these values would be valid one hundred years from now?

▪ Would you maintain these values even if they placed you at a competitive disadvantage?

▪ Would you take these core values to a new organization that you could start today?

If the group can identify a set of values for which they would all answer yes to these questions, then chances are good that these values do imbue the business. Next the group can identify the purposes of the company. Collins and Porras state that purposes should last 100 years! Usually the first statement of purpose that is offered is a reiteration of the business's product or service. For example, a group of physical therapists might say their purpose is to provide patient/client care. Collins and Porras recommend asking, 'Why is that important?' five times. By the time the group has answered "why" several times in a row, they will have arrived at a much deeper understanding of the purpose of the business (see "Asking Why" below).

That group of physical therapists may have arrived at the realization that their real purpose is actually to improve the health of their fellow neighbors or to better understand the affects of physical therapy on the human organism. Seldom in a successful company will the real purpose turn out to be making money.[11] In a successful company money is a means to an end, not the real purpose of the company. Collins and Porras say that choosing maximization of income as a core purpose is "a substitute—and a weak one at that."[11]

They also say that core ideology cannot be manufactured; it must be authentic. It also must be applied with discipline and consistency to all business decisions. Collins and Porras go so far as to say that if employees cannot adopt the core ideology, then they should not be retained. Instead the business should attract and retain only those employees who can share the core ideology with enthusiasm.

Asking Why

Original purpose:	To provide patient/client care
Why is that important?	Because people want to receive physical therapy
Why is that important?	Because people want to get better and be healthy
Why is that important?	Because being healthier contributes to a person's quality of life
Why is that important?	Because society does better if people are healthier
Why is that important?	Because a stronger society contributes to a sound future

Once a core ideology has been articulated, it is time to turn toward defining an envisioned future. An envisioned future is composed of two parts. First, a business should identify what Collins and Porras call "big, hairy, audacious goals" or BHAGs. BHAGs should be very long term—up to 20 or 30 years would not be unusual, especially if they are for the parent organization. Divisions of organizations may identify BHAGs that can be accomplished in 5 or 10 years. But the point is they have to be long term because they are so big and audacious, but they also should be clear and well defined, offering a definite finish line toward which people can aim. These BHAGS should then be translated into a vivid description so that all employees can relate to and work toward them enthusiastically.

It can be fun and exciting to bring people together to do this kind of visioning. It is important that people come ready to be reflective and futuristic. This is not the time for solving daily problems or setting specific short-range goals. It is helpful to set meetings for this kind of reflective activity apart from the routine management meetings that a business might have. Holding them in a different location, away from the interruptions of normal business often helps. It also can help to start the meeting with some unique activity that is symbolic of putting aside the normal frustrations, constraints, and personality conflicts to work collectively on these bigger issues. For example, the leader could pass out noise makers and encourage everyone to make as much noise as possible for 1 minute to drive out all mundane and frustrating thoughts, so that there will be plenty of room for creativity through out the meeting! This lighthearted approach sets the tone that the meeting will be different yet also clearly tells everyone to put aside day-to-day concerns to concentrate on long-term issues.

While Collins and Porras' work demonstrates that successful businesses have a shared, articulated vision, they also point out that it is the alignment of all business decisions with this vision that turns a grand vision into true success.

Mission

Accompanying a vision statement is a mission statement. The business must articulate the fundamental purpose that makes it different from other organizations of the same type. It must also articulate how it will operate and what goods or services it will generate. That statement, if it is truly meaningful, is the company's **mission**. A mission statement contains more concrete views than the vision statement, having grown from it.

Management Tip: Goals

Good organizations convey a strong vision of where they will be in the future. As a leader, you have to get your people to trust you and be sold on your vision. To sell staff on your organization's vision, you need to possess energy and display a positive attitude. No one wants to be stuck in a dead-end company going nowhere...or a company headed in the wrong direction. They want to be involved with a winner! And your staff members are the ones who will get you to that goal. A team with shared vision will be a more formidable competitor.

When setting goals, keep these points in mind:
1. Goals should be based on the basic mission and vision of the organization.
2. They should be realistic, attainable, and measurable.
3. They should improve the physical therapy practice (morale, financials, etc).
4. Staff should be involved in the goal-setting process.
5. A program should be developed to achieve each goal.

The mission statement should reflect the specific means that your business uses to accomplish its vision and seeks to do the following[12]:

- Clarify the organization's view of its long-term strategic position,

- Help to insure that the behavior of personnel is directed toward achievement of the mission,

- Convey a message to external stakeholders, such as investors, and

- Promote organizational confidence in top management.

The purpose of the mission statement is to:

- Provide the purpose of the organization,

- Express the philosophy that will guide the business,

- Articulate where the organization will be in the future (provides substance to the vision),

- Define the scope of the organization's activities, and

- Motivate employees through a clear sense of purpose and direction.

Key questions to ask in developing a mission statement are:

- What is the business?

- Who is the customer?

- What is of value to the customer?

- What will be the business?

- What should the business be?

- How will we treat each other?

Sample Mission Statements:

American Physical Therapy Association Section on Health Policy and Administration[13]
The purpose of the Section shall be:
To foster the development of leadership skills, empower members to influence health policy, legislation, and the regulation of physical therapy, and to serve as a resource to the APTA and its components in these areas.

American Physical Therapy Association[14]
The mission of the American Physical Therapy Association (APTA), the principal membership organization representing and promoting the profession of physical therapy, is to further the profession's role in the prevention, diagnosis, and treatment of movement dysfunctions and the enhancement of the physical health and functional abilities of members of the public.

Typical Physical Therapy Practice
XYZ Physical Therapy Practice will:
1. *Use evidence-based practice following the patient/client management model put forward by the APTA Guide to Physical Therapist Practice.*
2. *Make its services available to the diverse populations in our community, and provide pro bono services as part of its mission.*
3. *Strive to assure that all of its staff will have the best possible clinical skills, based on a sound program for professional development.*
4. *Interact with other providers in our community to provide coordinated care for our patients.*
5. *Provide clinical education for physical therapist students from ABC University.*

6.   *Participate in clinical research trials with faculty at ABC University.*
7.   *Provide sufficient income for wages, other fixed and variable costs, investment, and growth.*

XYZ's mission statement more clearly states the activities that are of value to this practice, further differentiating it from its competitors and providing a great deal of information about the core values of this group of physical therapists. Once these core values have been articulated, it becomes much easier to set measurable objectives with defined timeframes.

Objectives

The next step is to establish goals and objectives. Definable goals and objectives provide a way of measuring and evaluating movement toward achievement of the entity's vision. *Goals* outline what needs to be accomplished to reach the vision, and *objectives* specify the activities needed to achieve the goals.[15] Objectives are stated in precise, measurable terms.[16]

Sample goals and objectives:

American Physical Therapy Association Section on Health Policy and Administration[17]
Objectives:
A.   *Provide programs and opportunities for the exchange of information related to leadership, health policy, legislation, professional practice, regulatory issues and ethics.*

B.   *Promote and develop rehabilitation leaders in the areas of administration, health policy, regulation and ethics as they relate to the practice of physical therapy.*

C.   *Assist components of the Association, external groups, and agencies to enact and enforce appropriate legislation, regulation and rehabilitation management in order to benefit the profession of physical therapy and the people it serves.*

D.   *Enhance the practice of physical therapy by promoting active involvement in areas of leadership, legislation, regulation, and professional ethics.*

E.   *Encourage physical therapy research in the areas of health policy, administration, and professional practice, and foster contributions to professional literature related to these areas of physical therapy.*

American Physical Therapy Association[18]
Goal I: *Physical therapists are universally recognized and promoted as the practitioners of choice for conditions that affect movement, function, and health.*

> *Objective A: Ensure that physical therapists are recognized, valued, and utilized by consumers and other professionals as the practitioners of choice in the management of movement, function, and health.*

> *Objective B: Develop and implement strategies and activities that support members in exploring new practice opportunities and enhance their career prospects in the health care environment.*

> *Objective C: Facilitate the adaptation and expansion of practice to address the changing demographic composition of society.*

Typical Physical Therapy Practice Goals
1.   *Provide state-of-the art physical therapy to all clients.*
2.   *Provide access in scheduling appointment within 48 hours of referral.*
3.   *Promote delivery of physical therapy services to all clients, including provision of pro-bono services, within the financial abilities of the practice.*
4.   *Develop measurement systems to assure the delivery of evidence-based services.*

Tasks

The fourth step in success planning is to determine tasks, sometimes referred to as strategies and tactics. Through tasks, objectives are accomplished. Tasks are concrete, measurable events that must occur. An example might be: "The marketing manager will contact 150 potential referrers each month."

Timelines

The next step is to establish a priority for the tasks. Time is precious, and many tasks must be accomplished before another can begin, so establishing priorities helps to determine the order in which the tasks must be accomplished and by what date. For example: "Fifty physicians will refer patients for the first time by June 30."

Follow-up

The final step is to follow up, measure, and check to see if the business is doing what is required. The involvement of the business's leaders in this process serves to validate to all staff that the stated priorities are worthy of action, and thus that involvement is critical. It demonstrates on the leaders' part the commitment to see the matter through to a successful conclusion.

Planning Techniques

So far we have discussed two general approaches to the concept of planning: posing questions to more clearly define a business; and using the planning success cycle to develop vision, mission, values, goals, and objectives. Many, more specific approaches have been developed to use in devising a strategic plan. You may have read about one of these approaches or there may be a particular one that your facility or company has chosen to use.

Some other approaches that can be used include:[19]

- *Issue-based planning*, in which planners first identify and prioritize major issues for a business and then establish vision, mission, and objectives based on the issue(s) deemed most important.

- *Alignment planning*, in which planners identify areas or activities that need to be adjusted and incorporate needed changes as elements of the strategic plan. Alignment is useful for businesses that are experiencing problems with services, production, or efficiency and want to make improvements.

- *Scenario planning*, in which planners identify external influences on the business and develop scenarios (best-case, reasonable, and worst-case) based on those influences. Planners then develop potential responses to those influences and incorporate the most likely scenarios and responses into the strategic plan.

The most important issue is not which system you use, but that you do use a system, any system, to keep you on track with your planning. This section will discuss two ways to focus on identifying the strategies needed to accomplish the business vision and to assure that the strategies are implemented: the nominal group technique and SWOT.

Nominal Group Technique

One technique that can be very useful in a group setting to identify all possible strategies is known as either the Delbecq approach (named for Andre L Delbecq, who first described it) or the Nominal Group Technique.[20] This technique enables a group to generate and rank many ideas. It also assures that all members of the group have the chance to contribute equally and diminishes opportunities for destructive group behavior. To demonstrate the Nominal Group Technique, suppose the task at hand is to identify the strategies needed in the next 3 years to move the business closer to its vision, while meeting its current mission. The leader asks each group member to write down three different specific strategies. Next, each member of the group offers one item from his or her list. A recorder writes the items on a blackboard or flip chart as they are called out. The only discussion that occurs is to clarify the meaning of the item—there is no discussion about the value of the strategy in meeting the company's goals. The process is repeated until all participants have listed all of their items. If two people offer the same item a notation is made next to the item indicating that it has had a second nomination. By waiting until all items are listed before beginning discussion, the group centers on how to improve the item, rather than on the faults of the nominator. Once all the items have been finessed, the group ranks them. Ranking can be done in terms of importance, practicality, or another feature that meets the group's needs. By developing strategies in this way, the group has combined ownership of and buy-in to them; they are not seen as arising from a particular person. They also are clearly understood by all.

SWOT

Another technique that is widely used in planning is SWOT analysis.[21] SWOT stands for *strengths, weaknesses, opportunities,* and *threats* and is of primary value in the process of internal and external environmental scanning. It can also be used to determine the viability of a particular strategy or group of strategies. It requires that the people doing the analysis are willing to be completely honest, have a good grasp of the internal and external environment, and be willing to do information gathering.

The internal environment is analyzed first by determining a business's strengths and weaknesses. Strengths are the internal attributes that provide the resources needed to accomplish goals. These resources can be in terms of money, space, existing programs, or personnel. An example of a physical therapy practice's strengths may be the specific expertise of the clinical staff. It may be hardest to frankly describe a business's weaknesses, but inaccurate estimates of weaknesses can cause great damage to the potential success of a strategic plan. Sometimes it's easier to consider these as areas where improvements are needed. An example of a physical therapy practice's weaknesses may be frequent staff turnover.

Next, the external environment is analyzed by assessing opportunities and threats. Opportunities are situations that exist in the external environment that can be used to the business's advantage. They may be related to issues such as a lack of strong competitors, an upcoming demographic or regulatory change, or recent business merger. An example of an opportunity for a physical therapy practice may be the presence of a strong referral base. Threats are external situations that could have negative affects on the business. They may arise from issues such as limitations in reimbursement, business mergers, or regulatory changes. An example of a threat to a physical therapy practice may be competition from larger practices. As can be seen from these examples, similar activities in the external environment can have differing affects on a particular business at a particular time. One of the hallmarks of a success business is the ability to turn threats into opportunities. If performed accurately, SWOT analysis is truly a mechanism that helps reduce the risk of making uninformed decisions.

Project Management

Even the best-written plan will be a failure if it is not implemented successfully. Project management techniques can be very useful in helping to assure successful implementation of the plan. A *project* is a series of *tasks* or jobs undertaken by an individual manager or work team that require a significant amount of time to complete and are generally aimed toward some major output. Larger tasks may be divided into smaller units of work, or *subtasks*. Major-scale complex projects that may involve several years to complete are often called *programs*. Frequently the terms *project* and *program* are used interchangeably.

The major tasks that need to be monitored are time, cost, and resource availability.

Time. Among many advantages of project management is that it encourages a manager to think through the tasks and subtasks involved in the project ahead of time, identify their interdependencies, and put them into the correct sequence. Doing so allows for the orderly arrival of equipment or other materials and the proper scheduling for subcontractors and other services. One method of sequencing tasks is to view the sequence from the endpoint and work backward. As an example, consider a simple plan to revise treatment space with new partitions, floors, and treatment furniture:

Before the treatment tables may be placed in their areas, the flooring must be completed. Painting and plastering must be completed *before* the flooring contractor arrives. Wiring and plumbing need to be completed *before* the walls are closed up—as does a building inspection. *Before* each of those subtasks is undertaken, supplies need to be ordered and delivered. *Before* any task is even begun, the fire marshal may need to approve the plans, including the alarm system. If the premises are not suitable for the approval by the fire marshal, they may not be able to be certified for Medicare, if that is in the physical therapist's plans.

As we see, some things simply must be done before others. Building projects such as this one easily demonstrate the process because of their very tangible sets of tasks and subtasks, but the techniques are equally valuable for the development of a new service or the review of an existing one. It is much more efficient for a manager to think through the details first and then establish a rational plan for their accomplishment in the calm of the office than to do so in the midst of a busy project, when every step involves precious resources of time, people, materials, equipment, and money.

Cost. We have discussed money as a means to accomplish our vision and mission, and money has been identified as a resource necessary to accomplish many projects. It is therefore important to discuss the concept of budgeting, at least briefly. The term budget often is misused to refer to various financial statements or to the current financial state of the unit. But, a budget is actually just one more type of plan. Simply put, a budget lays out estimates of expenses, revenues, and income (revenues minus expenses) for a defined period of time. Managers then monitor the actual revenues and expenses against those predicted in the plan. With this definition in mind, we can see why a budget is an essential adjunct to a strategic plan.

Resource Availability. A manager also needs to identify the resources (people, space, equipment, money, etc) necessary for each task. If the resources are not readily available, some of the subtasks would include their acquisition.

Because project management can require a grasp of many, many details, several techniques have are available to help organize all of them. Two graphic techniques are used in critical path scheduling, Program Evaluation and Review Technique (PERT) and Critical Path Method (CPM).[22] Both techniques were originally designed to manage very large and detailed projects; PERT having roots

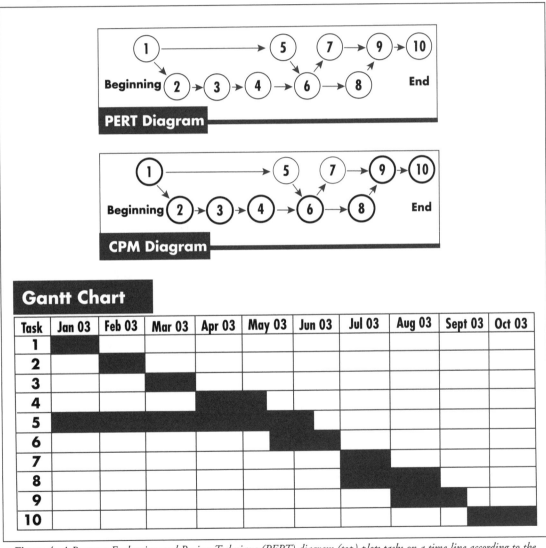

Figure 4. *A Program Evaluation and Review Technique (PERT) diagram (top) plots tasks on a time line according to the time needed to complete each task. By overlaying a Critical Path Method (CPM) diagram (center), the user can determine the time needed to complete the entire project. Finally, the user can place the tasks in a Gantt chart (bottom) to create a calendar showing the project start to finish.*

in the US Navy's development of the Polaris Missile Project and CPM having civilian roots at DuPont and Remington-Rand. However, they also are quite applicable to all sorts of activities, including implementation of a strategic plan, completion of office space planning, or hiring new employees.

PERT requires that the planners identify each task, determine the order in which the tasks need to be completed, and estimate the time needed for completion of each step. The tasks are plotted on a time line with the time to completion documented along the lines connecting each task. CPM overlays on the PERT chart the path that shows the maximum amount of time estimated to complete each task, thus identifying the time needed to complete the entire project. If this time is longer than that necessary for completion, the manager can identify the specific portions of the task where changes can be made. A manager can then use a Gantt chart to place the tasks in a column and show their start-to-end dates on a calendar. Figure 4 shows PERT and CPM diagrams and a Gantt chart for a simple activity. There are several software programs available to help a manager construct PERT and CPM diagrams and Gantt charts, including Microsoft Project©.*

Ethics

At first it might seem a bit odd to discuss business ethics in a chapter on strategic planning. But, remembering that a successful strategic plan must be derived from our most fundamental values, the link to ethics becomes obvious. Cynics may claim that the terms "business" and "ethics" are mutually exclusive, because there are so many public examples of apparently unethical behavior among business people. But, a discussion of ethics cannot be based solely on those who violate society's ethical norms, any more than it can be focused on the quality of health care solely on the instances of malpractice. Each is certainly a piece of the picture, but only a piece.

Ethics is a field of study, sometimes defined as a moral philosophy, that analyzes the morality of human conduct and values.[23,24] In common parlance, ethics has also come to describe the actual behavior itself. But it is useful to reflect that ethics is indeed related to the morality of behavior. This is not always a comfortable thought in a very secular world, but it simply means that when people think of ethics they are thinking of good and evil, or right and wrong.

Ethics actually deals with the choices people make among a range of behaviors that have varying degrees of being right or wrong. When people are faced with these choices, they face what is termed an "ethical dilemma." Much of ethical writing has been about guidelines for a process of ethical decision-making.

So what are the standards that help guide behavior in the business of physical therapy practice? Certainly, the ethical standards for direct patient/client care apply. In health care, four principles often are invoked for ethical conduct: autonomy, beneficence, nonmaleficence, and justice.[23] Over time, the value that society places on each of these principles may change. For example, 60 or 70 years ago, beneficence was primary, sanctioning paternalism among health care practitioners. Today, autonomy is a higher priority in society, leading to a much greater emphasis on informed consent and other patients' rights issues. The APTA *Code of Ethics*[25] is another useful standard for both personal and business decisions. APTA's *Standards of Practice*[26] have many implications for physical therapists' business behavior. In addition, legal and regulatory standards govern issues such as fraud and abuse and other illegal activities.

*Microsoft Corporation, Redmond, WA

None of these standards can give us unequivocal answers; indeed sometimes they actually seem to conflict with each other. At times like this it is necessary to use an ethical process.[23] Not surprisingly, this process bears a striking similarity to other planning or problem-solving processes:

- Define the problem, ensuring that the problem is indeed an ethical issue.

- Generate options for action.

- Identify the rights, duties, and obligations of all stakeholders, including external influences.

- Recognize and prioritize the conflicts among the options.

- Try some creative thought to seek a compromise.

- Choose and implement an action, and assess its outcomes.

By applying this process in a conscious manner, managers can identify the ethical implications of their strategies and make the choices that best match their ethical standards and values.

This still leaves the question of whether businesses have an obligation to make morally right decisions or whether they can actually be considered amoral. Drucker[1] says that businesses are made up of individuals, who do not leave behind their ethical obligations by virtue of being business leaders. So, the first answer to this question is that each member of an organization brings personal moral duties, obligations, rights, and values to his or her business activities. Just as visionary companies reflect the intellectual values of its members, successful companies will reflect the ethical values of its members.

Research by Jensen, Gwyer, Hack, and Shepard[2] has shown that expert clinicians exert a great deal of control over their practices. This is true for those who own their own practices as well as for those practicing in institutional settings. And one of the central values for many of these expert clinicians is a strong sense of moral obligation to their patients/clients, their community, and their profession. This sense of moral obligation showed itself

Deontologic vs Teleological

If a person holds to a *deontologic* (from the Greek for "duty") view of ethics, then the process of making ethical decisions may actually be quite easy, although living with those decisions may be more difficult. The reason that making the decision is relatively easy is that a deontologic approach to ethics says that there are certain duties and obligations that we have that derive from higher or fundamental sources and are always right. For example, for many people of certain cultures, the Ten Commandments represent absolute rules. If the Commandment says no to a certain behavior, than that behavior is simply wrong—a very straightforward decision-making process.

However, this approach does not always seem applicable to the complex situations of life. For example, one of the Commandments says, "Thou shalt not kill." But, many cultures have recognized that killing, as in war or self-defense, may sometimes be right, thereby removing the absolute certainty of the deontologic approach. Therefore another approach, termed the *teleological* (from the Greek for "end") approach has been proposed. In this view, the decision-maker needs to contemplate the consequences of his or her actions in making a choice. This is closely linked to a utilitarian approach, which says that the primary focus should be maximizing the greatest good for the greatest number. This approach means that decision-making can be far more complicated, although utilitarians still often turn to various rules or standards to help them in decision-making.

through the therapists' behavior. For example, these therapists left positions that did not meet patient needs adequately, even if it meant a personal monetary loss. They reported colleagues they knew to be violating professional ethics and legal standards. They made choices to provide pro bono care, including service overseas. They advocated for their patients by appealing every adverse insurance decision, as well as by working to affect health policy changes. They used this sense of moral obligation as they made pans for themselves and for their practices. For these experts, there is no distinction at all between their personal values and their professional or business values.

Conclusion

It should be clear that strategic planning does not exist in a vacuum. Rather, strategic planning is intricately entwined with many other management activities, including choice of management style, financial controls, and marketing. In addition, strategic planning is strongly linked to fundamental personal and professional values. A positive strategic planning process can be one of the most intellectually exciting and professionally satisfying activities in which managers can engage.

References

1. Drucker PF. *Management: Tasks, Responsibilities, Practices*. New York, NY: Harper and Row; 1974. (Reprinted by Harperbusiness; 1993).

2. Jensen GM, Gwyer J, Hack LM, Shepard KF. *Expertise in Physical Therapy Practice*. Boston, Mass: Butterworth-Heinemann; 1999.

3. Tversky A, Kahneman D. Judgment under uncertainty: Heuristics and biases. *Science*. 1974; 185:1124-1131.

4. Coulehan JL, Block MR. *The Medical Interview, 3rd ed*. Philadelphia, PA: FA Davis; 1997.

5. Section on Administration [now Section on Health Policy and Administration], American Physical Therapy Association. *Leadership, Administration, Management, and Professionalism*. Alexandria, Va: American Physical Therapy Association; 1998. Available at http://www.aptasoa.org. Accessed on December 16, 2002.

6. Guide to Physical Therapist Practice, 2nd Ed. *Phys Ther*. 2001;81:9-744.

7. Maslow AH. *Motivation and Personality*. New York, NY: Harper and Row; 1954.

8. Pfeiffer J, Jones JE. *A Handbook of Structured Experiences for Human Relations Training, Vol II*. Iowa City, Iowa: University Associates Press; 1974.

9. Section on Health Policy and Administration Vision Statement. American Physical Therapy Association Section on Health Policy and Administration. Available at http://www.aptasoa.org. Accessed December 16, 2002.

10. APTA Vision Sentence and Vision Statement for Physical Therapy 2020 (HOD 06-00-24-35). Alexandria, Va: American Physical Therapy Association; 2000. Available at http://www.apta.org/About/aptamissiongoals/visionstatement. Accessed on December 16, 2002.

11. Collins JC, Porras JI. Building your company's vision. *Harvard Business Review*. September-October 1996:65-77.

12. McGregor D. The Human Side of Enterprise. New York, NY: McGraw-Hill Book Co; 1960.

13. Section on health policy & administration. *The Health Policy Resource*. August 2002;2:23.

14. APTA Mission Statement (HOD 06-93-05-05). Alexandria, Va: American Physical Therapy Association; 1993. Available at http://www.apta.org/About/aptamissiongoals/aptamissionstatement. Accessed on December 16, 2002.

15. National School Boards Association. Education and leadership Toolkit/strategic planning tools. Available at http://www.nsba.org/sbot/toolkit/sgno.html. Accessed on October 18, 2002.

16. Longest B. *Management Practices for the Health Professional*, 4th ed. Norwalk, Conn: Appleton-Lange; 1990.

17. Section on health policy & administration. *The Health Policy Resource*. August 2002;2:23.

18. Goals That Represent the 2002 Priorities of the American Physical Therapy Association (HOD 06-01-06-09). Alexandria, Va: American Physical Therapy Association; 2001.

19. McNamara C. Basic Overview of Various Strategic Planning Models. Management Assistance Program for Nonprofits. Available at http://www.managementhelp.org/plan_dec/str_plan/models.htm. Accessed on October 18, 2002.

20. Delbecq AL, Van de Ven AH, Gustafson DH. *Group Techniques for Program Planning: A Guide to Nominal Group and Delphi Processes*. Glenview, Ill: Scott, Foresman and Company; 1975.

21. Nosse LJ, Friberg, DG, Kovacek PR. *Managerial and Supervisory Principles for Physical Therapists*. Baltimore, Md: Williams and Wilkins; 1999.

22. Walter J. *Physical Therapy Management, An Integrated Science*. St Louis, Mo: Mosby; 1993.

23. Swisher LL, Krueger-Brophy C. *Legal and Ethical Issues in Physical Therapy*. Boston, Mass: Butterworth-Heinemann; 1998.

24. Purtilo R. *Ethical Dimensions in the Health Professions*, 3rd ed. Philadelphia, Pa: WB Saunders; 1998.

25. APTA Code of Ethics (HOD 06-00-12-23). Alexandria, Va: American Physical Therapy Association; 2000. Available at http://www.apta.org/PT_Practice/ethics_pt/code_ethics. Accessed on December 16, 2002.

26. APTA Standards of Practice for Physical Therapy (HOD 06-00-11-22). Alexandria, Va: American Physical Therapy Association; 2000. Available at http://www.apta.org/PT_Practice/For_Clinicians/Standards/Standards. Accessed on December 16, 2002.

Additional Readings

Anthony R, Govindarajan V. *Management Control Systems*. Boston, Mass: Richard D. Irwin; 1995.

Brown S, Eisenhardt K. *Competing on the Edge: Strategy as Structured Chaos*. Boston, Mass: Harvard Business School Press; 1998.

Chase RB, Aquilano NJ. *Production and Operations Management*, 7th ed. Boston, Mass: Richard D Irwin; 1995.

Clemen RT. *Making Hard Decisions*, 2nd ed. Boston, Mass: Duxbury Press; 1996.

Feinberg M, Tarrant JJ. *Why Smart People Do Dumb Things*. New York, NY: Fireside/Simon & Schuster; 1995.

Finkler S. *Finance and Accounting for Non-financial Managers*. Englewood Cliffs, NJ: Prentice-Hall; 1992.

Frunzi GL. *Supervision, The Art of Management*. Englewood Cliffs, NJ: Prentice-Hall; 1991.

Henry D. *The Profitable Professional Practice*. Englewood Cliffs, NJ: Prentice-Hall; 1985.

Hamel G, Prahalad CK. *Competing for The Future*. Boston, Mass: Harvard Business School Press; 1994.

Ginter PM, Swayne LM, Duncan WJ. *Strategic Management of Health Care Organizations*. Malden, MA: Blackwell Publishers; 1998.

Kotler P. *Marketing Management: Analysis, Planning, Implementation, and Control*, 8th ed. Englewood Cliffs, NJ: Prentice-Hall; 1994.

Kotter JP. *Leading Change*. Boston, Mass: Harvard Business School Press; 1996.

McDonald J. *Strategy in Poker, Business, and War*. New York, NY: WW Norton; 1996.

Maister DH. *Managing the Professional Service Firm*. New York, NY: Free Press; 1997. Maister DH. *True Professionalism*. New York, NY: Free Press; 1997.

Megginson L, Mosley D, Pietri P. *Management: Concepts and Applications*, 3rd ed. New York, NY: Harper and Row; 1989.

Montgomery CA, Porter ME. *Strategy: Seeking And Securing Competitive Advantage*. Boston, Mass: Harvard Business Review; 1991.

Morehead G, Griffin R. *Organizational Behavior: Managing People and Organizations*. Boston, Mass: L Houghton, Mifflin & Company; 1995.

Pearce JA, Robinson RB. *Strategic Management: Formulation, Implementation, and Control*, 5th ed. Boston, Mass: Richard D Irwin; 1994.

Raia A. *Managing By Objectives*. Glenview, Ill: Scott, Foresman and Company; 1974.

Rumelt RP, Schendel DE, Teece DJ. *Fundamental Issues in Strategy*. Boston, Mass: Harvard Business School Press; 1994.

Russo EJ, Schoemaker PJH. *Decision Traps: The Ten Barriers to Brilliant Decision-Making and How to Overcome Them*. New York, NY: Simon & Schuster; 1990.

Schneidler B, Bowen D. *Winning the Service Game*. Boston, Mass: Harvard Business School Press; 1995.

Senge PM. *The Fifth Discipline: The Art And Practice Of The Learning Organization*. New York, NY: Currency Doubleday; 1994.

Velasques MG. *Business Ethics*, 3rd ed. New York, NY: Simon & Schuster; 1992.

Wolper LF. *Health Care Administration: Principles, Practices, Structure, and Delivery*, 2nd ed. Gaithersburg, Md: Aspen Publishers; 1995.

Welsh G, Hilton R, Gordon P. *Budgeting: Profit Planning And Control*. Englewood Cliffs, NJ: Prentice-Hall; 1988.

White TK. *The Technical Connection*. New York, NY: John Wiley & Sons; 1981.

Chapter 4

Strategic Management

Definition of Management

There are many definitions of "management." Management is the process of obtaining, deploying, and utilizing a variety of essential resources in support of an organization's objectives.[1] Management is working with and through other people to accomplish the objectives of both the organization and its members.[2] It is the achievement of organizational objectives through people and other resources. The manager's job is to combine human and technical resources in the best way possible to achieve these objectives.[1] A simple, yet valuable, definition is that management is the process of getting things done through people.[2]

Why is Management Important?

Management is critical to the success of any organization,[2-3] for it provides the formal leadership for the organization.[3] Managers influence the specific operations of the practice. In physical therapy, managers have significant input into the clinical practice patterns of the clinicians. Managers also work to enhance and develop the skills and success of the staff. Most importantly, management personnel work to assure that the organization's objectives are being accomplished.

The Management Pyramid

Organizations typically are structured to follow a hierarchical relationship.[4-6] The levels of management are top management, middle management, and supervisory management.[4] These layers are referred to as the management pyramid (Figure 1).

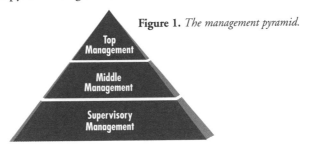

Figure 1. *The management pyramid.*

Top management includes executives who develop long-range plans and interact with the public, board members, and other stakeholders.[1]

Middle management is more involved than top management in specific operations within the organizations.[2] Middle managers are responsible for developing detailed plans and procedures to implement the general plans of top management.[1]

Supervisory, or firstline, management includes people who are directly responsible for the details of assigning employees to specific jobs and evaluating immediate performance.

Figure 2 gives examples of organizational structures for a simple and a more complex organization. Table 1 presents typical titles within physical therapy organizations as they fall into each level of the management pyramid.

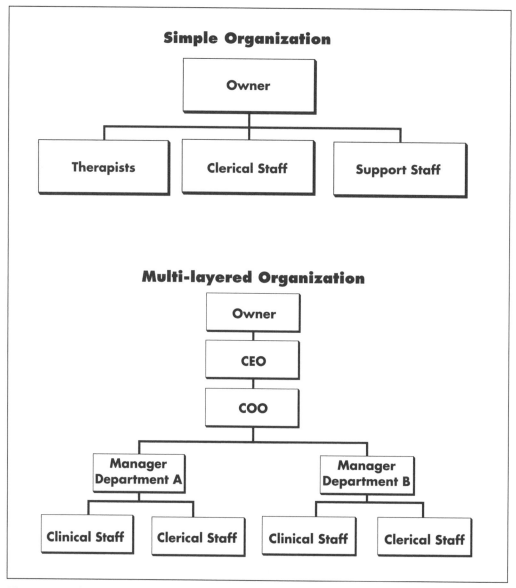

Figure 2. *Simple and multi-layered organizational structures.*

	Small Physical Therapy Organization	Integrated Delivery System
Top Management	Owner, Chief Executive Officer (CEO), Chief Operating Officer (COO), Chair of Corporate Board	Administrator, Chief Executive Officer (CEO), Chief Operating Officer (COO), Chair of Corporate Board
Middle Management	Site Director, Manager	Department Head, Director, Manager
Supervisory Management	Supervisor	Supervisor, Team Leader, Lead Therapist

Table 1. *Typical Titles in Physical Therapy Organizations.*

The combination of an organization's structure, function, and personnel typically determine the ultimate success or failure of a practice. Failure in any one of these three areas will virtually assure failure or demise of the practice. Success in all three will create an environment in which organizational goals can be accomplished.

Who Should Manage?

There are many tasks that every physical therapist does in the course of a typical day that require strong management skills. Management skills are required of all physical therapists—not just those with the title of manager.[7]

In working with patients, physical therapists must incorporate strong listening, coaching, counseling and performance evaluation skills into the hands-on clinical care that is provided to the patient. In situations in which staff therapists oversee the work of physical therapist assistants, aides, technicians, or students, strong management and delegation skills are needed.

To function effectively enough in today's financially charged environment, every clinician must be able to use strong business and management skills to effectively assist the patient/client in the most cost-effective manner in the context of the patient's financial constraints. These constraints usually include restrictions on the type or amount of therapy services that are covered by insurance programs and the personal financial resources of the patients themselves. Whether or not it is agreed to be appropriate and desirable, clinical management of patients is strongly influenced by the business environments in which physical therapists practice.

To be effective in the clinical care of patients, every therapist must be competent in the business aspects of the profession. This requires a strong professional development plan that begins with the professional education program and continues throughout the clinician's career. Every therapist should include components of management, business skills acquisition, and leadership development in his or her career plan.[7]

Management is not an optional component of a physical therapist's professional life; it is a core behavior.[7] Clearly the answer to the question "Who should manage?" is that all physical therapists should and do manage and thus must be sure to have adequate management skills to succeed.

Management Skills

Every manager must possess certain characteristics in order to succeed. The general areas of these skills are technical skills, human relations skills, and conceptual skills. Depending on the requirements of the specific managerial position, the mix of these three sets of skills will vary.

Technical Skills

Technical skills refer to the manager's ability to understand and use the techniques, knowledge, and tools of a specific discipline or department.[1] Technical skills are particularly important for supervisory (firstline) managers who are frequently involved with production employees. In physical therapy, technical skills include those skills that are unique to the delivery of physical therapy services, ie, clinical interventions. For "clinician managers" in physical therapy, demonstration of technical skills is critical to gaining the respect of staff with whom the supervisor works.

Physical Therapists as Managers—Or Not?

Managers of physical therapy services may or may not be physical therapists. In many situations, especially in larger integrated delivery systems, physical therapy services have been bundled into business units called product or service lines. These service lines may be rehabilitative services or other more patient-focused service lines, such as orthopedic or neurologic services. In these situations, a physical therapist may or may not be the manager of the business unit.

There are special considerations when physical therapy services are not managed directly by a physical therapist. Clearly, regardless of the academic or clinical preparation of the manager, non-physical therapist managers must be very knowledgeable about physical therapy services. They should be open to learning about physical therapy from others, including those they manage. They also must be careful not to direct clinical decisions that fall only within the domain of a physical therapist. An interesting situation arises when the non-PT director of a service line assists a physical therapist in clinical activity. Unless the director is a physical therapist assistant, he or she can function only as an aide—directly under the close supervision of the physical therapist in matters related to clinical care. In many states, aides are not legally able to provide any clinical services other than routine housekeeping and general assistive activities. This can be quite a role reversal for the non-PT department manager. One minute he or she supervises the physical therapist; the next minute the same physical therapist is supervising the manager/aide. Conflict can easily arise.

There are distinct advantages when the manager of a rehabilitation service line is a physical therapist, including knowledge, understanding, and acceptance. But in order for a physical therapist to successfully step into the role of manager—at any level—she or he must be both motivated to that role and adequately prepared to manage. In some, if not most, situations, the physical therapist may wish to pursue additional formal training (via continuing education in business areas such as this home study course or via an advanced business degree) to prepare for success as a manager of physical therapy services.

Interpersonal Skills

Interpersonal skills, also referred to as human relations skills, are "people" skills involving the manager's ability to work effectively with and through people.[1] They relate to communicating with, leading, and motivating employees, and are important at all levels of management.

Of all interpersonal skills, communication may be the most important. As Figure 3 shows, it is at the center of several key characteristics of good management. Communication is the exchange and flow of information and ideas from one person to another.[8-13] Studying the communication process is important managers coach, coordinate, counsel, evaluate, and supervise through this process. It is the chain of understanding that integrates the members of a practice from top to bottom, bottom to top, and side-to-side.

What is involved in the communication process?

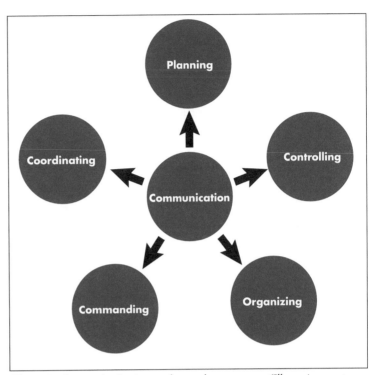

Figure 3. *Communication is central to good management. (Illustration courtesy of the author. ©2002 by Peter R Kovacek.)*

- First, information exists in the mind of the sender. This can be a *idea*, concept, information, or feelings.

- Next, a message is sent to a receiver in words or other symbols (the message is *encoded*).

- And finally, the receiver translates the words or symbols into a concept or information (the receiver *decodes* the message).

During the transmitting of the message, the receiver receives both content (the actual words or symbols of the message) and context (the way in which the message is delivered, such as tone of voice, the look in the sender's eye, body language, or state of emotion).

Many managers think that they have communicated once they have told someone to do something. But the truth is that a message has not been communicated unless the receiver *understands* it.

How does one know when a message has been properly received? By two-way communication or feedback. Feedback will tell the sender that the receiver understood the message, its level of importance, and what must be done with it. Communication is an exchange, not just a delivery of thought processes by a sender. All parties must participate actively in order to complete the information exchange.

Good feedback requires effective listening. Hearing and listening are not the same thing. Hearing is the act of perceiving sound. It is involuntary and simply refers to reception of aural stimuli. Listening is a selective activity that involves reception and interpretation. It involves decoding the sound into meaning.

Listening may be passive or active. Passive listening is little more than hearing. Active listening, on the other hand, involves listening with purpose. It may be done to gain information, obtain directions, understand others, solve problems, share interests, see how another person feels, or show support. It requires that the listener attend to the words and the feelings of the sender for understanding. Active listening takes the same amount of energy or more, than does speaking. It requires the receiver to hear the various messages, understand the meaning, and then verify the meaning by offering feedback.

Conceptual Skills

Conceptual skills relate to the ability to see the organization as a unified whole and to understand how each part of the overall physical therapy practice interacts with the other parts.[1] Simply put, it is the ability to see the "big picture." This is particularly important for individuals in the higher ranks of management who are most responsible for the overall direction of the organization, including the development of organizational mission and vision statements (described later in this chapter).

The importance and level of use of these three skills will vary depending on the situation and the level of management at which one is practicing (Figure 4).

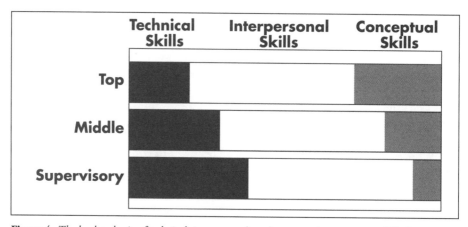

Figure 4. *The level and mix of technical, interpersonal, and conceptual management skills that managers need differs among top, middle, and supervisory positions and can vary depending on a particular situation.*

Supervision

Supervision is the act of keeping a grasp on a situation and ensuring that plans and policies are implemented properly. It includes giving instructions and inspecting the accomplishment of a task. Because this is an area of significant controversy within physical therapy practice, physical therapist managers should refer to APTA's positions on the use of personnel, accessible on the Association's Web site at www.apta.org/PT_Practice. From the screen, click "Information for Clinicians," then "Use of Personnel (Supervision)." Adequate supervision requires a delicate balance to ensure that neither over-supervision (micro-management) nor under-supervision (neglect) prevails. Over-supervision stifles initiative, fosters resentment, and lowers morale and motivation. Under-supervision often leads to miscommunication, lack of coordination, and the perception by subordinates that the manager does not care. Both managers and staff members benefit from appropriate supervision.

Evaluation is a critical part of supervising. Evaluation involves judging the worth, quality, or significance of staff, ideas, or things, and it includes looking at the ways in which people accomplish a task. For the person being evaluated, it means getting feedback on how well something is being done and interpreting that feedback. Without feedback, employees are more likely to continue to perform tasks incorrectly or to stop performing the steps that lead to success.

Hersey, Blanchard, and Johnson developed a model[5] that aids the manager in providing the appropriate level of training/coaching and motivation. Good managers provide training, coaching, and motivation depending on the learning level of their employees. The process follows a pattern similar to this:

1. A person learns a new task. She or he is enthusiastic to learn a new skill but may be somewhat apprehensive because she or he is about to enter a *change process*. The learner needs lots of clear instructions (training), because the task is new, and just a little bit of emotional support (motivation) to calm the stress of change.

2. In the second step, the level of guidance lessens, so that the learner may experiment somewhat with the learning style that works best for him or her. The learner has now failed a few times in the process, so while instruction lessens, emotional support increases to keep the learner's confidence high.

3. At the next level, the learner has become capable of performing the new skill. The amount of instruction drops to just a few pointers so that the learner can experiment with the new skill. But the learner is still not confident. The amount of emotional support increases to build up confidence. At this point, the manager is more of a coach than a trainer.

4. Toward the end of the learning process, the employee knows the job. The manager provides very little coaching so that the employee can begin to take ownership of tasks and responsibilities. The employee is allowed to perform with little or no direction. Now the manager delegates, as the employee is encouraged to take on new responsibilities and new assignments. Then the cycle repeats itself with new tasks.

Training and Coaching

Training and coaching are two different things, although the terms are often used interchangeably. "Training" is a structured lesson designed to provide the employee with the knowledge and skills to perform a task. "Coaching," on the other hand, is a process designed to help the employee gain greater competence and to overcome barriers in order to improve job performance.

Training and coaching help create the conditions which will assist someone to learn and develop. People learn by the examples of others, by forming a picture in their minds of what they are trying to learn, by gaining and understanding necessary information, by applying it to their job or practice.

Counseling

Counseling can have a powerful, long-term impact on staff and the effectiveness of an organization. Counseling is talking with a person in a way that helps that person solve a problem or helps to create conditions that will cause the person to improve behavior. It involves thinking, implementing, knowing human nature, timing, sincerity, compassion, and kindness. It involves much more than simply telling someone what to do about a problem.

Managers must demonstrate the following qualities in order to counsel effectively:

- **Respect for employees.** This is based on the belief that individuals are responsible for their own actions and ideas. It includes an awareness of a person's individuality through unique values, attributes, and skills. As managers attempt to develop staff through counseling, they must refrain from projecting their own values onto employees.

- **Self-awareness.** This is an self-understanding of the manager. The more managers are aware of their own values, needs, and biases, the less likely they will be to project their feelings onto employees.

- **Credibility.** This is achieved through both honesty and consistency between the manager's statements and actions. Credible managers are straightforward with their employees and behave in such a manner that staff respect and trust their words.

- **Empathy.** This entails understanding a staff member's situation. Empathetic managers are better able to help subordinates identify a negative situation and develop a plan to improve the situation.

The goal of counseling is to help employees grow and develop in their ability to achieve organizational or individual goals. At times counseling may be directed by policy; and at other times, managers choose to counsel to develop employees. Regardless of the nature of the counseling, the manager should demonstrate the qualities of an effective counselor (respect, self-awareness, credibility, and empathy) and employ strong skills of communication (see page 37).

While the reason for counseling is to develop staff members, managers often categorize counseling based on the topic of the session. Major categories include performance counseling, problem counseling, and individual growth counseling. While these categories may help to organize and focus counseling sessions, they must not be viewed as separate and distinct types of counseling. For example, a counseling session that focuses on resolving a problem may also have a great impact on improving job performance, and a counseling session focused on performance may also include a discussion of opportunities for growth.

There are two types of counseling: directive and nondirective. In directive counseling, the counselor identifies the problem and tells the counselee what to do about it. In nondirective counseling, the counselee identifies the problem and determines the solution with the help of the counselor. The counselor must determine which of the two, or what appropriate combination, to use in each situation.

Regardless of the topic of the counseling session, managers should follow the same basic format to prepare for and conduct counseling, using these steps as a guide:

1. Identify the problem. Ensure that you really know what the problem is.
2. Analyze the forces influencing the behavior. Determine which of these forces you can control and which forces the employee controls. Determine if the forces must be modified, eliminated, or enforced.
3. Plan, coordinate, and organize the session. Determine the best time to conduct the session so that you will not be interrupted or forced to end too early.
4. Conduct the session using sincerity, compassion, and kindness. This does not mean that you cannot be firm or in control. Your reputation is on the line—the problem must be solved so that your department can continue with its mission. But you must hear the person out.
5. During the session, determine what the employee believes to be the cause of, for example, counterproductive behavior and what will be required to change it. Also determine if your initial analysis of the problem is correct.
6. Try to maintain a sense of timing of when to use directive or nondirective counseling.
7. Using all the facts, make a decision and/or develop a remediation plan of action to correct the problem. If more counseling is needed, set a firm time and date for the next session.
8. After the session, and throughout a sufficient time period following, evaluate the employee's progress to ensure that the problem has been resolved.

Hints for Counseling Sessions

1. Let the person know that the behavior (not the person) is undesirable.
2. Let the person know that you care about him or her as a person but that you expect performance at the level of the employee's capabilities.
3. Do not discipline employees who are unable to perform a task. Reprimand those who are able to perform the task but are unwilling or unmotivated to succeed.
4. Reprimand in private soon after the undesirable behavior. Do not humiliate a person in front of others.
5. Ensure that the employee understands exactly what behavior led to the reprimand.
6. Do not hold a grudge after reprimanding. When a counseling session is over...it's over.

Performance Appraisals

The performance appraisal is one of the most powerful employee behavior modification tools available to a manager. It has three main objectives:

1. To measure performance fairly and objectively against job requirements. This allows effective employees to be rewarded for their efforts and ineffective employees to be put on the line for poor performance.

2. To increase performance by identifying specific development goals. The appraisal allows the employee to target specific areas for job growth. It should be a time to plan for better performance on the job.

3. To develop career goals so that the employee may keep pace with the organization's requirements. Just because an employee is performing effectively in his or her job now does not mean that he or she will be able to perform effectively in the future. The employee must be allowed to grow with the job and the physical therapy practice.

A staff member should not walk blindly into a performance appraisal. Past counseling sessions and feedback should give the employee a clear understanding of what to expect from the appraisal. Managers who surprise their employees have not done their jobs.

The appraisal should be a joint effort. No one knows the job better than the person performing it. By turning the appraisal into a real discussion, the manager may gain insights that could help boost performance in the future. Before the meeting, the employee should complete a self-appraisal. Although some managers are concerned that employees will take advantage of this by giving themselves unearned high marks, many employees actually are more critical of themselves than is their manager!

Management versus Leadership

While motivating employees in the pursuit of organizational goals is a function of management, influencing them toward those goals requires leadership. Although the terms "management" and "leadership" often are used interchangeably, they are distinct. The important difference is the way in which each serves organizational goals. Leadership occurs whenever there are attempts to influence individuals or groups, whether for personal or organizational goals.[5,8,14-15]

Some forms of leadership exist in all groups, with a central attribute being social influence. The leader is the person who has the most impact on a group's behavior and beliefs, whether formally appointed or not.

The functions of leadership are many and varied, depending on the basic problem that a group must deal with, and the type of leadership style in action, which is dependent on the leader's basis of power.[8,9,12-17]

Power, in the case of leadership, may be viewed in four categories that are interrelated:

- *Expert power* is concerned with skills, knowledge, and information that the holders of such abilities are able to use to influence others (eg, technicians and computer personnel).

- *Coercive power* involves the ability to either reward or punish the person being influenced in order to gain compliance.

- *Legitimate power* is conferred by the very role structure of the group or organization itself and is accepted by all as correct and without dispute (eg, the ranks assigned to members of the military or police).

- *Referent power* involves identification with the leader by those being influenced (eg, rock or film personalities using their images to enter the political arena).

Most managers make use of a combination of these four types of power, depending on the leadership style used. Authoritarian leaders, for example, use a mixture of legitimate, coercive, and expert powers, to dictate the policies, plans, and activities of a group. In comparison, a democratic or participative leader would use primarily referent power, involving all members of the group in the decision-making process.

Most people view leadership as being associated with the role of a manager, but just as "leadership" and "management" are not synonymous, neither are "leader" and "manager." Leading and managing involve separate and distinct behaviors and activities. Leaders and managers may vary in their orientation toward goals, conceptions about work, interpersonal styles, and self-perceptions. Another way to view the distinction is that managers fulfill four functions: planning, organizing, controlling, and motivating. The leadership aspect of management involves influencing employees toward achievement of organizational goals. A manager may not necessarily be a group's leader. While the manager of a group performs activities of a planning, organizing, and controlling nature, the real leader may be one of his or her employees. These informal leaders often possess abilities that appointed managers might lack, such as technical expertise or communication skills. An effective manager will incorporate these informal leaders into their operations for the achievement of organizational goals. Leadership is particularly critical in times of stress, such as during organizational change.

Styles of Leadership

Leadership style is the manner of and approach to providing direction, implementing plans, and influencing people. These three different leadership styles are most often cited: authoritarian (autocratic), participative (democratic), and delegative (free reign).

Which Style When

A good manager uses a variety of leadership styles, depending on what forces are involved among the followers, the leader, and the situation.[5] Examples include:

- Using an authoritarian style with a new graduate who is just learning to be a physical therapist. The manager is competent and a good coach. The new graduate is motivated to learn a new skill. The situation is a new environment for the new graduate.

- Using a participative style with a team of experienced staff members who know their jobs. The manager knows the problem well, but wants to create a team in which the employees take ownership of the project. The employees know their jobs and want to become part of the team. The situation allows time.

- Using a delegative style with a senior physical therapist who knows more about the specifics of the situation.

- Using all three: The manager tells staff that a procedure is not working correctly and a new one must be established (authoritarian). He or she asks for their ideas and input for creating a new procedure (participative). The manager then delegates tasks in order to implement the new procedure (delegative).

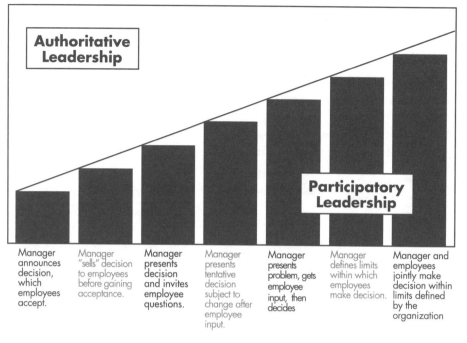

Authoritative Leadership

Participatory Leadership

| Manager announces decision, which employees accept. | Manager "sells" decision to employees before gaining acceptance. | Manager presents decision and invites employee questions. | Manager presents tentative decision subject to change after employee input. | Manager presents problem, gets employee input, then decides | Manager defines limits within which employees make decision. | Manager and employees jointly make decision within limits defined by the organization |

Figure 5. *Continuum of manager-employee behavior. The shift from authoritative to participative leadership styles is characterized by increasingly interactive communication between manager and employees. (Adapted by permission of* Harvard Business Review. *From "How to Choose a Leadership Pattern" by Tannenbaum R and Schmidt W, May-June 1973. ©2002 by the Harvard Business School Publishing Corporation; all rights reserved.)*

Authoritarian (autocratic). An authoritarian leader tells employees what needs to be done and how it should be done, without getting input or advice from the employees. This style is most appropriately used when the leader has all the information necessary to solve the problem and employees are well motivated. Although some people equate this style with yelling, using demeaning language, or leading by threats and abuse of power, that behavior is not the authoritarian style but simply abusive, unprofessional business behavior.

When time is adequate and the leader wants to gain more commitment and motivation from employees, then a more participative style should be considered.

Participative (democratic). In this style, the leader includes one or more employees in determining what to do and how to do it. However, the leader maintains the final decision-making authority. This is not a sign of weakness; it is a sign of strength that employees will respect. The democratic style is best used when the leader and employees each have some of the information required for decision-making. This style allows employees to become part of the team and allows the leader to make informed decisions with more employee buy-in.

Delegative (free reign). In this style, the leader allows the employee(s) to make decisions but retains responsibility for the decisions that are made. The delegative style is most workable when employees are able to analyze situations and determine what needs to be done and how to do it. The leader cannot do everything and often must set priorities and delegate certain tasks. This style requires the leader's trust and understanding of individual employee abilities.

Tannenbaum and Schmidt[18] expanded this concept into further specificity of style when they described seven alternatives for communication and leadership styles, as illustrated in Figure 5. It is evident the amount and interactive nature of communication between the leader and the team progressively increases in moving from an authoritarian to participative style.

References

1. Boone LE, Kurtz DL. *Contemporary Business, 7th Ed.* New York, NY: Dryden Press; 1993.

2. Drucker PF. *The Practice of Management.* New York, NY: Harper Business; 1954.

3. Montana PJ, Charnow BH. *Management, 2nd Ed.* Haupauge, NY: Barrons; 1993.

4. Hodge BJ, Anthony WP. *Organization Theory, 2nd Ed.* Boston, Mass: Allyn and Bacon Inc; 1984.

5. Hersey P, Blanchard KH, Johnson DE. *Management of Organizational Behavior—Utilizing Human Resources, 7th Ed.* Upsaddle River, NJ: Prentice Hall; 1996.

6. Hampton DR, Summer CE, Webber RA. *Organizational Behavior and the Practice of Management, 4th Ed.* Glenview, Ill: Scott, Foresman and Co; 1982.

7. Section on Administration [now Section on Health Policy and Administration], American Physical Therapy Association. *Leadership, Administration, Management and Professionalism.* Alexandria, Va: American Physical Therapy Association; 1998. Available at http://www.aptasoa.org. Accessed on December 16, 2002.

8. Laborde GZ. *Influencing with Integrity—Management Skills for Communication and Negotiation.* Palo Alto, Calif: Syntony Publishing; 1983.

9. Dilenschneider RL. *Power and Influence: Mastering the Art of Persuasion.* New York, NY: Prentice Hall; 1990.

10. Ouchi W. *Theory Z: How American Business Can Meet the Japanese Challenge.* Reading, Mass: Addison-Wesley; 1981.

11. Skinner BF. *Science and Human Behavior.* New York, NY: The Macmillan Company; 1953.

12. Decker B. *You've Got to Be Believed to be Heard.* New York, NY: St Martin's Press; 1992.

13. Cohen AR, Bradford DL. *Influence Without Authority.* New York, NY: John Wiley and Sons; 1989.

14. Schatz K, Schatz L. *Managing by Influence.* New York, NY: Prentice Hall; 1986.

15. Pfeffer J. *Managing with Power—Politics and Influence in Organizations.* Boston, Mass: Harvard Business School Press; 1992.

16. Swets PW. *The Art of Talking So That People Will Listen—Getting Through to Family, Friends and Business Associates.* New York, NY: Simon and Schuster; 1983.

17. Fisher R, Ury W, Patton B. *Getting to Yes—Negotiating Agreement Without Giving In, 2nd Ed.* Boston, Mass: Houghton Mifflin; 1992.

18. Tannebaum R, Schmidt WH. How to choose a leadership pattern. *Harvard Business Review.* May-June 1973.

Chapter 5

Schools of Management Theory

Why Is It Important to Understand Management Theory?

Management theory involves attempts to understand how people behave in a work environment. Because the primary job of a manager is to accomplish tasks through the work of others,[1] theories that can help explain the behavior of employees in relation to managers can have a significant impact on the competitive position of the physical therapy organization.[3, 6-7, 17-19] Additionally, as has been illustrated frequently throughout history, "Those who cannot remember the past are condemned to repeat it."[8]

The study of management theory allows managers to step back and understand situations from an academic perspective. This process helps managers consider the basis for management decisions, rather than merely relying on their own personal experience or the anecdotal evidence of others.

Additionally, management theory and practice continues to evolve. Being knowledgeable of this evolution is beneficial to managers on a daily basis.

There are several different schools of thought on the process of management:
1. Classic school
2. Behavioral school
3. Management science school
4. Contingency school

The Classic School: Scientific Management

Scientific management is based on the work of **Frederick Taylor**,[9] who is best known for his time and motion studies. Scientific management also is referred to as the classical, scientific, traditional, or rational schools.[10] Scientific management involves the development of systematic processes, management principles, and measurement and analysis of the tasks and activities that take place at work in an effort to improve work output.

Frederick Taylor[9] is said to be the father of scientific management, method study, and work measurement and incentive payments systems that link work outputs directly to levels of reward. In the introduction to his 1911 book, *The Principles of Scientific Management*, Taylor states, "In the past the man has been first; in the future the system must be first."

His work drew together his fascination with organizations dominated by managerial ideas and actions. He argued that he was applying "scientific" method to practical management problems. His principles—which reflect a systematic study of work behavior and his views on the direct relationship between incentives and employee efforts—are evident today in modern organizations, even though much of his work is contradicted by evidence relating to employee behavior.

Scientific management forms of regulation (piecework, incentives, and bonuses) continue to be used by managers. Taylor's management devices, particularly work measurement and job specialization, have decisively influenced 20th century work. His models are based on assumptions about a "typical, economically motivated" employee linked to notions of employee/management relations and enterprise as a social organization.

Central to Taylor's work is a set of beliefs about work and employees that is referred to as Theory X. The basic beliefs of Theory X are:

- Employees are alienated from their work.
- Employees wish to avoid high levels of effort.
- Employees are motivated solely or largely by pay.
- Employees distrust management.

In addition to Taylor, several other theorists were prominent in the development of the classic school of management theory.

Henry Gantt[2] was an associate of Taylor. Gantt's contributions are in the areas of scheduling of tasks and in employee reward programs. Today, in many areas of work enhancement and project management, Gantt charts are commonplace. Gantt's approach included a systematic representation of tasks and time frames for completion of projects. Figure 1 provides an example of a Gantt chart for a simple project.

Henri Fayol[11] was the first significant theorist to expand management theory into organizational theory by addressing not just issues related to how employees are supervised, but also issues related to optimal systems and structures across an entire enterprise. Fayol differentiated supervision from management by defining the functions of management—planning, organizing, coordinating, and

	10/21/03	10/22/03	10/23/03	10/24/03	10/25/03	10/26/03	10/27/03	10/28/03
Define goals	●							
Assemble team		●						
Train team			●					
Acquire raw materials				●				
Prepare final product					●			
Inspect product						●		
Evaluate performance							●	
Adjust operations								●

Figure 1. *Simple Gantt chart.*

controlling. He also believed that managers must be flexible in their approach and *learn* the best practices to apply in each specific situation. Fayol described 14 key principles of "classic management" that are presented below.

1. *Division of labor* refers to the manner in which work is separated into specific tasks and divided among employees or groups who are specialized or highly competent in the specific tasks.
2. *Authority* is the right to exercise power within an organization to direct employees. Responsibility is closely linked, and includes the accountability to use authority.
3. *Discipline* is the shaping of behavior of employees through the use of incentives and disincentives. Discipline is usually thought of from the perspective of punishment – either real or perceived.
4. *Unity of command* is the concept of "single master," where each employee is responsible to answer to and report to only one supervisor.
5. *Unity of direction* implies that the organization is consistent in its mission and vision of its future.
6. *Subordination of the individual* is the belief that the needs of the overall organization should carry a higher rating and is more important than the needs of any individual within that organization.
7. *Remuneration* concepts require that individual employees be compensated according to general principles that are applied to all employees within the organization. Typically the factors considered in determining compensation are qualifications of the employee, employment market forces of supply and demand, performance of the employee, and the general economic climate for the organization.
8. *Centralization* is the concentration of power, authority, and decision-making in a single location. The principle of centralization suggests that managers should be able to delegate responsibility with a commensurate level of authority to carry out the delegated task with out the manager losing overall responsibility for the activity.
9. *Chain of command* refers to the stratification of authority and responsibility within an organization, where managers who are higher in an organization structure supervise managers who are lower in the organization structure. First-level managers supervise the employees.
10. *Order* describes the concept of assuring that the resources, both human and material, of the organization are appropriately deployed to allow efficiency.
11. *Equity* describes the concept that there is relative justice and fair treatment of all employees within an organization. The organization's work rules, policies, and procedures often assure equity.
12. *Stability of personnel* refers to the concept of adequate recruitment of new employees and successful retention of existing employees so that consistency in work processes and relationships is maintained.
13. *Initiative* is seen in a self-motivated work force. Motivation from external sources, although possible, is much less likely to achieve work objectives as efficiently as self-motivated work.
14. *Esprit de corps* is a sense of harmony and shared interest by the employees. The end result is strong relationships among the work force including both managers and employees.

The primary implications of the classic school of management are a greater reliance on established company policies and procedures and on prescribed relationships in formal work groups. Given the developing industrial organizations of the late 1800s and early 1900s, these schools met the needs of their time. However, as modern-day organizations and employees have evolved, so has management theory.

The first evolution away from the classic school was the behavioral school, or human relations model, of management theory.

The Behavioral School: Human Relations Model

This school of management thinking was based on the belief that an understanding of human behavior will get employees to cooperate and be productive toward the organization's goals. As much as the classic school focused on the work, the behavioral school focused on the employee.

The behavioral school is a social science or human relations model of how work is accomplished. Much of the behavioral school rose out of experiments that Elton Mayo conducted at Western Electric Company's Hawthorne Plant between 1927 and 1932. These seminal experiments became known as the "Hawthorne experiments," And the response that was identified became known as the "Hawthorne effect."

Elton Mayo[12] was a social scientist who attempted to identify physical environment factors that affect work output. After a lack of success with classical school interventions at a textile plant, Mayo suggested that managers attend to employees' perceived needs and wants as a means of increasing productivity. When management followed Mayo's suggestions, the textile plant's productivity rose, turnover fell, and morale improved. To further his study of employee impact on work, Mayo moved on to the Hawthorne Plant, where he implemented a series of trials in which the lighting was altered in a highly stressful part of the plant to determine the impact of illumination on productivity. A control group was established in which no lighting changes were made.

Surprising results were found. There was no consistent relationship between illumination and productivity. Mayo believed that employees increased productivity because:

- Employee-supervisor relations were more relaxed in the test room,

- The test room was an enjoyable work environment,

- Employees liked being involved in the experiment,

- Employees were more productive because they were observed and measured, and

- Participating in the experiment increased the feeling of group identity and belonging.

There was a general feeling that the very act of measuring performance seemed to improve that performance. In effect, employees behaved as they were measured. Mayo termed these sorts of factors of productivity "human relations factors." For the first time, management theory considered the individual employee and workgroup in addition to the tasks and structures of the workplace.

The behavioral school does not disprove the classic school; it recognizes that classic school considerations are important but not sufficient to describe all aspects of the production of work.

Another behavioral school theorist, **Chester Barnard**,[13] put forward the acceptance theory of authority that states that individuals form organizations to accomplish a common set of goals that require a cooperative effort for success. However, employees determine if a manager's authority is legitimate and acceptable based on the individual employee's understanding of the manager's action in the context of the organization's goals. It was first recognized that a manager's power comes not from the position of manager, but rather from the support of common objectives by the employees. This was in strong contrast to the classic school, which held that the manager possessed an absolute power based purely on assignment to the position of manager.

Douglas McGregor[14] is the last of the behavioral school theorists to be discussed here. McGregor recognized that if the work of Mayo and Barnard was valid, the assumptions of Taylor and other classical theorists related to Theory X couldn't describe all employees.[3] McGregor identified an alternative to Theory X, which he called Theory Y.

McGregor's Theory Y suggests that:

- Employees have the potential for development, the capacity for assuming responsibility, and the readiness to work for organizational goals.

- Management makes it possible for employees to recognize and develop positive traits.

Table 1 compares Theory X and Theory Y, contrasting differing behavioral concepts.

Implications of the Behavioral School

The behavioral school:

- Promotes decentralization, delegation, job enlargement, empowerment, participation, and self-management, and it suggests that more intense delegation of authority to lower organizational levels is desirable.

Theory X	Theory Y
Employees are lazy, indifferent to needs of the organization, and not interested in doing a good job.	Employees will respond to good working conditions by doing a good job.
Employees care only about their own needs.	Common goals are important to employees.
Employees must be persuaded, rewarded, controlled, and directed for success.	Employees can be self-motivated and self-directed if they are committed to the organization's objectives.
Employees have limited intellectual capacity.	Employees' full capacity is rarely fully used.
Employees will resist change.	Employees can be creative and adaptive.

Table 1. *Comparison of Theory X and Theory Y.*

- Places a high priority on designing jobs and tasks in such a way that they will allow the employee to be challenged.

- Suggests that more job responsibility for all employees will enhance productivity.

- Encourages creative reward systems for work well done.

- Suggests that increased flow of information to the lower levels of an organization will increase work output.

- Requires that employees be treated with respect.

Management Science School: Quantitative Approach

The management science school, also known as the quantitative approach to management,[3,4,10] evolved out of the need to rapidly bring the US industrial complex to maximum production during World War II. This approach is based on the application of scientific methods to problems of production in the work place. There is a heavy emphasis on mathematics and careful numeric analysis of work place problems.

There are four steps of the scientific process used in the management science school (Figure 2)[1,5-6]:
1. Management observes the problem as a scientist would.
2. A mathematical model of the system is constructed.
3. The model is used to draw conclusions about parts of the production systems that cannot be easily observed.
4. The model is used to test various alternative actions through a series of experiments.

Clearly the contribution of the management science school is that it emphasizes the use of numbers and relies on mathematics and statistics. It is the quantitative science of business management. But, as Albert Einstein said, "Not everything that counts can be counted, and not everything that can be counted, counts." There is the potential to gain a false sense of security from the quantitative aspects of the business analysis. However, as a supplement to the previous theories, it provides an additional perspective to many business problems.

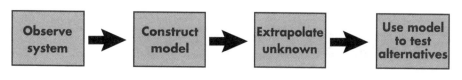

Figure 2. *The four steps of the management science approach.*

An additional concept of scientific management is the matching of tasks to individual employees through job design. Job design is the specification of the content and methods of jobs or tasks; it also is known as work design, job structuring, or work structuring. Job design is based on four key concepts in scientific management:

- Task specialization

- Chain of command

- Unity of direction

- Span of control

Task specialization involves the narrowing of job tasks to include only those that can truly be mastered.[3] It often involves reduction of tasks by an employee and may lead to over-simplification of a task. Chain of command refers to the reporting relationships within an organization. Unity of direction is the sharing of common goals by all individuals and working units of the organization. Span of control is the number of individuals any specific manager or supervisor must oversee or supervise.

Other concepts central to scientific management are:

- Job analysis
- Job enhancement
- Job enrichment

Job analysis is the systematic process of uncovering and describing the components of a job or task.[16] Job enhancement (or job enlargement) is expanding the scope of a job. It is the opposite of task specialization. Job enrichment is expanding a job's content to provide employees with increased opportunity to experience personal responsibility and meaning at work and to obtain more information about the outcome of the work. It is similar to, but not the same as, job enhancement. (See further discussion of job enhancement and job enrichment is Chapter 7, Motivation, under "A Hierarchy of Needs.")

Contingency School

The contingency school of management theory suggests that there is no universally acceptable explanation for all contemporary work-related behaviors. Further, it suggests that the realities of each situation will determine the most appropriate course of analyzing organizational behavior. Although the contingency school may, at first glance, seem rather unstructured and random, it identifies specific steps to determine the best approach to finding the preferred management solution. The decision steps of the contingency school as identified by Montana and Charnov[2] are:

1. Conduct situational analysis of internal and external conditions.
2. Formulate a statement of the problem.
3. State performance standards in a measurable, observable, and relevant manner.
4. Generate alternative solutions.
5. Evaluate possible solutions related to anticipated success.
6. Select best alternative(s).
7. Test proposed solution.
8. Revise as needed.
9. Implement solution.
10. Evaluate the result.
11. Revise the process as needed.

As you can tell from the above decision steps, the contingency school borrows techniques from a variety of management theories. Because it does not limit the thought process to any predetermined beliefs about the work or the employee, the contingency school allows a thorough analysis and structured decision-making process. As such it may be the most likely of all the management schools to lead to an optimal action plan.

References

1. Drucker PF. *The Practice of Management.* New York, NY: Harper Business; 1954.

2. Montana PJ, Charnow BH. *Management, 2nd Ed.* Haupauge, NY: Barrons; 1993.

3. Hersey P, Blanchard KH, Johnson DE. *Management of Organizational Behavior—Utilizing Human Resources, 7th Ed.* Upsaddle River, NJ: Prentice Hall; 1996.

4. Hampton DR, Summer CE, Webber RA. *Organizational Behavior and the Practice of Management, 4th Ed.* Glenview, Ill: Scott, Foresman and Co; 1982.

5. Bittel LR, Newsstrom JW. *What Every Supervisor Should Know, 6th Ed.* New York, NY: McGraw-Hill; 1990.

6. Dilenschneider RL. *Power and Influence: Mastering the Art of Persuasion.* New York, NY: Prentice Hall; 1990.

7. Zuker E. *The Seven Secrets of Influence.* New York, NY: McGraw-Hill; 1991.

8. Santayana G. *The Columbia World of Quotations.* New York, NY: Columbia University Press; 1996. Available at http://www.bartleby.com/66/. Accessed on October 8, 2002.

9. Taylor FW. *The Principles of Scientific Management.* New York, NY: Harper & Bros; 1911.

10. Hodge BJ, Anthony WP. *Organization Theory, 2nd Ed.* Boston, Mass: Allyn and Bacon Inc; 1984.

11. Fayol H. *Industrial and General Administration.* Paris: Dunod; 1925. Translated by JA Coubrough, Geneva International Management Institute; 1930.

12. Mayo E. *The Human Problems of an Industrial Civilization.* New York, NY: The Macmillan Co; 1933.

13. Barnard CI. *The Functions of the Executive.* Cambridge, Mass: Harvard University Press; 1938.

14. McGregor D. *The Human Side of Enterprise.* New York, NY: McGraw-Hill Book Co; 1960.

15. Boone LE, Kurtz DL. *Contemporary Business, 7th Ed.* New York, NY: Dryden Press; 1993.

16. Cooper CL, Argyris C. *The Concise Blackwell Encyclopedia of Management.* Malden, Mass: Blackwell Publishers; 1998.

Chapter 6

Additional Concepts

Theory Z

After World War II, there was significant opportunity to study management theory during the reconstruction of several of the most devastated countries. One of those most closely studied was Japan. **William Ouchi** is a management scientist who studied the Japanese management processes as the country arose from the ashes of Hiroshima and Nagasaki and grew into a power in the world economy. Ouchi described these Japanese management processes as Theory Z.[1]

The management of Theory Z organizations is characterized by[2]:

- Long-term employment,

- Intensive socialization of the workforce,

- Objectives and values emphasize cooperation and teamwork,

- Employees are expected to be generalists rather than specialists,

- Performance appraisal systems are complex,

- Emphasis is on workgroups rather than on individuals,

- Open communication,

- Consultative decision making,

- Relationship-oriented concern for employees, and

- Greater centralization than in Theory X organizations.

Another key component of Theory Z organizations is an emphasis on quality of work life (QWL). This is often seen in American organizations as quality circles, total quality management, or continuous quality improvement processes. QWL is related to the richness of the job environment. Its purpose is to develop jobs and working conditions that are excellent for both the employees and the organization. One way to accomplish QWL is through job design or redesign, as explained in the Management Science School discussion on page 52.

Management Concept	McGregor (Theory X & Y)[3]	Ouchi (Theory Z)[1]
Motivation	Tends to categorize people as one type or another: either unwilling or unmotivated to work, or being self-motivated toward work. Threats and disciplinary action are thought to be more effective in this situation, although monetary rewards also can be a prime motivator to make Theory X employees produce more.	Believes that people are innately self-motivated to do their work, are loyal toward the company, and want to make the company succeed.
Leadership	Theory X leaders are more authoritarian, while Theory Y leaders are more participative. In both cases, the managers retain a great deal of control.	Theory Z managers trust that their employees can make sound decisions. Therefore, this type of leader is more likely to act as a "coach" and to let the employees make most of the decisions.
Power and Authority	McGregor's managers would seem to keep most of the power and authority. In the case of Theory Y, the manager takes suggestions from employees, but retains the power to implement the decision.	The manager's ability to exercise power and authority comes from the employees trusting management to take care of them and allowing them to do their jobs. The employees have a great deal of input and weight in the decision-making process.
Conflict	This type of manager might be more likely to exercise a great deal of "power" based on conflict resolution style, especially with Theory X employees. Theory Y employees might be given the opportunity to exert "negotiating" strategies to resolve their own differences.	Conflict in the Theory Z arena would involve a great deal of discussion, collaboration, and negotiation. The employees solve the conflicts, while the managers play more of a "third-party arbitrator" role.
Performance Appraisals	Appraisals occur on a regular basis. Promotions occur on a regular basis.	Theory Z emphasizes more frequent performance appraisals but slower promotions.

Table 1. *Comparison of Management Theorists McGregor and Ouchi.*

The key components of Theory Z processes are:

◼ Greater employee involvement in decision-making,

◼ Improved and more intense communication between employees and management,

◼ Self-direction of employees and work groups, and

◼ High levels of management support for the concept of quality improvement.

Table 1 provides a comparison of Theories X and Y and Theory Z.

Management by Objectives

Another more recent management practice is management by objectives (MBO).[4] This involves an interactive process between manager and subordinate whereby they jointly:

◼ Identify and agree upon the subordinate's work goals,

■ Define each of their responsibilities for achieving agreed-upon goals, and

■ Use goal accomplishment as a guide for examining and evaluating the subordinate's performance.

The primary advantage of MBO is that it provides a mechanism for the organization to be consistent in its approach to developing performance objectives and evaluating performance. Activities and plans developed using MBO techniques require that top management clearly articulate organizational objectives and that all levels of management base specific action plans and performance objectives on the organization-wide objectives.

All employees and their managers, in setting and providing regular feedback on these objectives, base MBO on specific, objective, measurable, and challenging objectives and intimate participation.

Change Management

Few organizations are isolated from change, and so change management is a central theme in many management actions. A manager's style may take on an entirely different dimension when applied to change management.

In a static situation, ie, one in which there is no change, the need for management is much less than when conditions are dynamic, erratic, or evolving. Regardless of the degree of change required, management is the process of accomplishing work through others.[4] As such, it requires adaptation and adjustment by all members of the work force, including managers.

Within groups of individuals who need to respond to change, there are several areas that could require adjustment. These are: knowledge, attitudes, individual behavior, and group behavior. Figure 1 illustrates each of these areas weighted by its typical prevalence, difficulty in achieving, and time required to change.

	Prevalence	Difficulty	Time Involved
Knowledge	●	○	○
Attitudes	●	◒	◒
Individual behavior	◒	◒	◒
Group behavior	◒	●	●

Figure 1. *Four areas that require adjustment during times of organizational change are knowledge, attitudes, individual behavior, and group behavior. Each area is weighted by its typical prevalence, difficulty in achieving, and time required to change. An open circle indicates a lower prevalence, less difficulty, or less time required to resolve. A darkened circle indicates a higher prevalence, more difficulty, or more time required to resolve. A partially filled circle indicates a middle position for each area.*

Why Change?

Today's physical therapy world is highly competitive. The way to survive is to reshape the organization to match the needs of a rapidly changing world. Resistance to change is futile...for managers and their businesses. Patients and referral sources not only demand excellent service, they also demand more value, meaning they expect more for less money. If you do not supply it, your competitors will. Physical therapy organizations are reshaping themselves to change quickly to meet the needs of their customers. Managers need to emphasize action to make the change as quickly and smoothly as possible—although not hastily.[5]

The Japanese use the term "kaizen," meaning continual improvement. This is a never-ending quest to do better. Standing still allows competitors to get ahead.

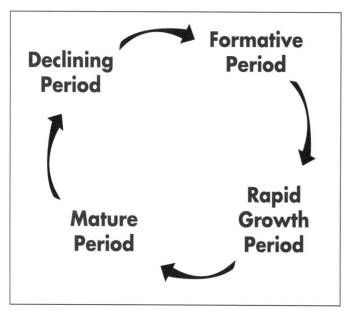

Figure 2. *The typical organizational lifespan includes four phases: a formative period, a period of rapid growth, a mature period, and a period of decline.*

Organizations go through four principal phases in their life span (Figure 2)[4,6,7]:

Formative Period. The formative period represents the startup of a new organization. Although there is a founding vision—why the organization was started—there are no formal definitions. This is just as well; there is often much learning, experimentation, and innovation taking place. These changes of creativity and discovery are needed to overcome obstacles and accomplish breakthroughs.

Rapid Growth Period. During the rapid growth period, direction and coordination are added to the organization to sustain growth and solidify gains. Organizational change is focused on defining the purpose of the organization and on the mainstream business.

Mature Period. As the organization matures, growth levels off to the overall pace of the economy. Organizational changes are needed to maintain established markets and assure that maximum gains are achieved.

Declining Period. For many organizations, the declining period means downsizing and reorganization. Changes must include establishing difficult objectives and compassionate implementation of action plans. The goal is to get out of the old and into something new. Success in this period occurs when the organization is able to start the cycle over again.

For some organizations, the four periods of growth come and go very rapidly. For others, it may take decades. Failure to follow through with needed changes in any of the four growth periods may often mean the death of the organization.

Change Acceptance

Throughout periods of change—which occur nearly constantly in good organizations—managers must concentrate on helping their employees to evolve from change avoidance or resistance through change and to, finally, acceptance and commitment. Figure 3 illustrates the four stages of change acceptance.[8]

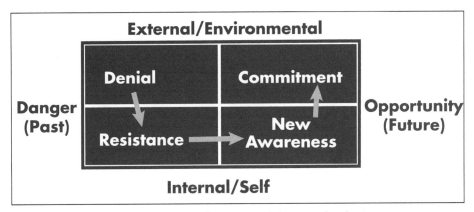

Figure 3. *The four steps toward acceptance of organizational change are denial, resistance, new awareness, and commitment.*

These stages are similar to Kubler-Ross's description of the stages of acceptance of death.[9] And change within an organization is not unlike the death of a close friend. That is why many employees' or individual's reaction to change is to first deny and then resist it. People become comfortable performing tasks in a certain way. This comfort provides them with the security that they are in control of their environment. They fear that change could disrupt their routines, make their

Management Tip: Leading the Change

Martin Luther King did not say, "I have a very good plan"; he shouted, "I have a dream!" A successful leader provides passion and a strong sense of purpose of the change. Passion is contagious. When someone is passionate about something, it is inspiring. Create change so that others want to be part of it. When you give them a part in it, you also must give them the authority and control to act upon it. Share the power so that they do not feel powerless. You want them to feel useful and enthusiastic. Convince them that the change could not happen without them, and that they are needed.

jobs harder, or cause them to lose a sense of control, and so on. The manager needs to recognize his or her employees' stage of acceptance and serve as a guide through periods of change.

References

1.   Ouchi W. *Theory Z: How American Business Can Meet the Japanese Challenge*. Reading, Mass: Addison-Wesley; 1981.

2.   Cooper CL, Argyris C. *The Concise Blackwell Encyclopedia of Management*. Malden, Mass: Blackwell Publishers; 1998.

3.   Hersey P, Blanchard KH, Johnson DE. *Management of Organizational Behavior—Utilizing Human Resources, 7th Ed*. Upsaddle River, NJ: Prentice Hall; 1996.

4.   Drucker PF. *The Practice of Management*. New York, NY: Harper Business; 1954.

5.   Larkin TS, Larkin S. *Communicating Change—How to Win Employee Support for New Business Directions, 2nd Ed*. New York, NY: McGraw-Hill; 1994.

6. Montana PJ, Charnow BH. *Management, 2nd Ed.* Haupauge, NY: Barrons; 1993.

7. Hodge BJ, Anthony WP. *Organization Theory, 2nd Ed.* Boston, Mass: Allyn and Bacon Inc; 1984.

8. Kovacek PR. *Managing Employees in Changing Times.* Harper Woods, Mich: KMS; 1996.

9. Kubler-Ross E. *On Death and Dying.* New York, NY: Touchstone; 1997.

Chapter 7

Motivation

Motivation is the process of stimulating an individual to take action that will accomplish a desired goal.[1] Motivation theory seeks to understand, explain and predict:

- Which of many possible goals an individual chooses to pursue.
- How much effort an individual will exert to pursue a goal.
- How long an individual will pursue a goal.

In management terms, motivation refers to an important management activity—the techniques used by managers to facilitate employee actions that lead to the accomplishment of organizational goals.

According to Nosse et al,[2] motivation is a psychological construct term that reflects biological, interpersonal, and social needs that people strive to fulfill. Typically, motives are not directly observable except as they influence behavior. Behaviors are actions that are undertaken, supposedly to fulfill an unmet human need (ie, a motive). Because the motive isn't necessarily observable, researchers over the years have developed several theories about how and why employees are motivated.

A Hierarchy of Needs

Abraham Maslow's Hierarchy of Needs Theory[3] suggests that only unfulfilled needs are real sources of motivation. Maslow identified five need levels that are hierarchical in nature, that is, they range from primitive and immature (physiologic and safety) to civilized and mature (ego-status and self-actualization). He theorized that employees become aware of and are concurrently motivated by each of the unfulfilled needs in ascending order, as shown in Figure 1. The lower levels are concerned with basic survival needs and the higher levels with the realization of human potential.

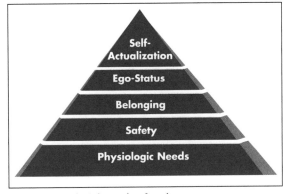

Figure 1. *Maslow's hierarchy of needs.*

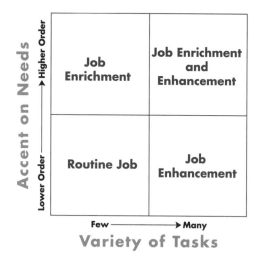

Figure 2. *The effects of job enrichment versus job enhancement on performance. A job is enhanced by adding a variety of tasks to avoid monotony, while a job is enriched by adding responsibilities that satisfy an employee's higher-order needs, as described by Maslow's hierarchy of needs.*

The implications for physical therapy managers of the hierarchy of needs theory is that managers should attempt to recognize the appropriate level of motivation for each employee and develop systems and supports to enable individual employees to satisfy their specific needs.

The concepts of job enhancement and job enrichment (introduced in Chapter 5 under "Management Science School: Quantitative Approach") could be applied to the lower-level versus higher-level needs defined by Maslow. Remember, job enhancement adds a greater variety of tasks and duties to the job so that it is not as monotonous, taking in the *breadth* of the job (ie, the number of different tasks that an employee performs). Job enrichment, on the other hand, provides additional motivators. It adds *depth* to the job (ie, more control, responsibility, and discretion as to how the job is performed). This satisfies the higher-order needs of the employee, rather than simply adding variety. Figure 2 illustrates the differences.

The benefits of job enrichment are many, including:

- Growth of the individual.

- Greater job satisfaction of the Individual.

- Self-actualization of the individual.

- Better employee performance for the organization.

- Organization gets intrinsically motivated employees.

- Less absenteeism, turnover, and grievances for the organization.

- Owners and employees prosper.

- Full use of human resources for society.

- Society gains more effective organizations.

There are a variety of methods for implementing job enrichment:

- **Skill Variety.** Perform different tasks that require different skills. This differs from job enlargement, which might require the employee to perform more tasks but requires the same set of skills.

- **Task Identity.** Create or perform a complete piece of work. This gives a sense of completion, responsibility, and pride in a job well done.

- **Task Significance.** Impact that the work has on other people from the employee's perspective.

- **Autonomy.** Gives employees discretion and control over job-related decisions.

- **Feedback.** Information that tells employees how well they are performing. It can come directly from the job (intrinsic task feedback) or verbally from someone else (extrinsic feedback).

Implementation of job enrichment and job enhancement for physical therapists must always include consideration of the details that are unique to the situation.[4] The purpose of these actions

Are You Sliding Down Maslow's Hierarchy?

(Revised with permission, Kovacek[5])

Abraham Maslow's Hierarchy of Needs Theory suggests that only unfulfilled needs are real sources of motivation. Maslow identified five hierarchical need levels—physiologic, safety, belonging, ego-status, and self-actualization—that range from primitive and immature (physiologic and safety) to civilized and mature (ego-status and self-actualization). This means that people become aware of and are concurrently motivated by each of the unfulfilled needs in ascending order. The lower levels are concerned with basic survival needs and the higher levels with the realization of human potential.

Physical therapy managers therefore should attempt to recognize the appropriate motivating level for each employee and develop systems and supports to assist them in satisfying their specific needs. Maslow was not a PT. Possibly, he never met a PT or even heard of physical therapy. But there is much more going on in physical therapy these days that Maslow's theory can explain. So let's step back a bit from the daily grind. Let's look at what is happening in our industry from the eyes of Maslow.

Our Recent Past

In the past 20–30 years, physical therapy, as a profession, has seen rapid growth and incredible development. Physical therapists have been well regarded in our communities, we have been well paid for very interesting work, and all of the groups that monitor such things have endorsed physical therapy as a great profession. Certainly, getting into PT school was difficult and getting out even more challenging, but once we had that license we had a ticket to the profession—with jobs a plenty, great salaries, good working conditions, and employers who, at least at times, treated us with respect and reverence.

In Maslow's language, our physiologic and safety needs were pretty well covered by Level 1 and 2 on the hierarchy just by having that license and doing our jobs well. We had food on the table and good living conditions thanks to the high demand for therapists and plentiful salaries. One of the other advantages to being a PT has been that the people we work with were generally very nice, caring, hard-working folks. We quickly found a strong sense of community among other therapists. We were proud to be physical therapists. In Maslow's terms, we were satisfying our need for "belonging"—Level 3 in the hierarchy.

When we think about the work that we did as therapists, we were truly blessed. We have had the privilege of working with patients and clients who really needed us, and they usually appreciated us, too. Not all professionals can say that the work that they do *every day* matters—ours did, and so we took great pride in our work. Maslow refers to this as satisfying our need for ego and status—Level 4 of the hierarchy.

So where did this leave us? At the top level of Maslow's hierarchy is self-actualization. Maslow defines self-actualization as the need for fulfillment, for realizing one's own potential, for using totally one's talents and capabilities. As the US Army says, "Be all that you can be!" Self-actualization is pretty heady stuff. There are not a lot of rules on how to maximize your potential. We spent a lot of time developing ourselves. Our patients, our employers, and our selves all benefited from these lofty aspirations.

"Oops, I Slipped on a Pile of Self-Actualization!"

Self-actualization seeking feels pretty good. In fact, many consider it intoxicating. At the very least, seeking our highest levels of functioning consumes our time, our thoughts, and our energies. However, several key things have changed.

There probably are no longer have more jobs than therapists—at least in many parts of the country. Our salaries no longer automatically rise just because we have lasted another year on the job. Many outside our profession seem to be questioning our value to the health care system and to our patients. Instead of calls from recruiters looking to give us jobs, we get calls from colleagues who are looking for a "good" job. We seem to spend as much time on the business side of the physical therapy as we do on the clinical care of our patients. Everyone seems a bit crabbier and less fun to be around at work, too.

The US health care industry has changed, and we are being changed with it. We don't usually like having change imposed on us, and this time is no different. We struggle with all these changes. They all seem so distracting—from our patients, from our work, from our pursuit of personal enhancement.

As we stand at the pinnacle of Maslow's pyramid, we rarely realize how precariously we were perched. It does not take a lot to dislodge us and down we slide. First we are dislodged from our high esteem, then our co-workers are angry and we lose our sense of belonging. Next friends or co-workers take pay cuts or lose jobs. Maslow would say we are back at the bottom levels of the hierarchy. Or are we?

Maslow describes what happens in typical situations. But maybe Maslow never met a physical therapist—intelligent, creative, resilient, hard working, right-minded, and caring. Although we have taken some hits in the pocket book and prestige arena lately, we need to focus on some of the things that still remain. Our patients are still benefiting from what we do. We still can find ways to enjoy what we do so well. We have tremendous resources to learn alternative ways to provide incredibly high quality of care to those who need us so much.

is to enhance performance and work. Care must be taken to discuss the proposed managerial actions with the affected staff members. Table 1 provides examples of job enrichment and enhancement for several job categories in a typical physical therapy practice.

Hygiene vs Motivation Factors

Frederick Herzberg[6] examined motivation from a different, but not contradictory, perspective than that of Maslow. While Maslow examined motivation in general, Herzberg focused on work and workplace motivational issues. Herzberg put forth what has become known as the Motivation/Hygiene or Two-Factor Theory of Motivation, by which he identified two distinct issues that seem to affect workplace motivation.

Herzberg's "hygiene factors" included:

- Organization policy
- Administration
- Working conditions

- Interpersonal relationships on the job

- Salary

- Status

- Job security

As the list above illustrates, hygiene factors are similar to several of the lower-level needs that Maslow identified. One key to hygiene factors that is important for managers to understand is that in the worst of situations, hygiene factors can lead to significant dissatisfaction. In the most ideal situations, however, hygiene factors will not motivate; rather, they will only end dissatisfaction (Figure 3).

Employee	Job Enhancement	Job Enrichment
Physical Therapist	Expand job to include both adult and pediatric patients/clients. Expand job to include intervention with acute care and home care patients, instead of just one or the other.	Enrich job to include not only evaluation and intervention with a specific patient/client population, but also design of community-based educatioonal programs for that same population. Enrich job to include assessment of clinical outcomes for the entire clinic related to a specific population of patients/clients.
Physical Therapist Assistant	Expand job to include assisting with more complicated or sophisticated interventions (as permitted by practice act). Expand job to include completion of financial forms with the patient/client.	Enrich job to include being a reserch assistant for a clinical trial in the practice. Enrich job by being an instructor in the PTA program at the local community college.
Clerical Staff Member	Expand job to include set-up and clean-up for clinical care. Expand job to include phone coverage for another department or practice during lunch hours.	Enrich job by assisting in the design of clerical forms or intake proceses. Enrich job by supervising other clerical staff members
Physical Therapist Supervisor	Expand job by widening the span of control by having more staff report directly to the supervisor. Expand job by supervising an additional clinic or site.	Enrich job by designing the departmental outcome process. Enrich job by additional training in quality improvement and participation in organization-wide accreditation preparations.

Table 1. *Job Enhancement vs Job Enrichment for Selected Physical Therapy Positions.*

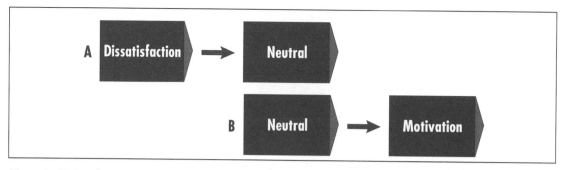

Figure 3. *Hygiene factors versus motivation factors. Hygiene factors (A) are similar to Maslow's lower-level needs and, according to Herzberg, merely will end dissatisfaction but not encourage employees to maximize their performance. Motivation factors (B) are similar to Maslow's higher-level needs and, according to Herzberg, are needed to maximize employees' work performance.*

Herzberg also identified "motivation factors." These include:

- Achievement
- Recognition
- Work itself
- Responsibility
- Advancement
- Growth

All employees are motivated, but differ by what motivates them most. The items on this list are similar in many ways to the factors at the higher levels of Maslow's hierarchy. These factors, according to Herzberg, are those that lead to truly motivated employees. In pursuit of these factors, employees will enhance their work performance, becoming more productive and better able to meet organizational goals.

Herzberg's theory also recognizes the potential for changes in what motivates employees at different stages of the employee's life and in different economic conditions.

Theory X/Y in Motivation Theory

As mentioned in Chapter 5 under "The Behavioral School: Human Relations Model," Douglas McGregor's[7] opposing theories of Theory X and Theory Y offer different perspectives of employees and their interaction with work and the organization. Remember that each suggests different explanations for employee's behavior in the workplace and different sets of plausible managerial actions to accomplish work. Theory X suggests that managers need to coerce, cajole, and control employees in order to accomplish organizational objectives. Theory Y suggests that employees are responsible and merely require leadership—not control—to accomplish the work of the organization.

McClelland's Theory of Motivation

According to David McClelland,[8] writing in 1961, three important specific motives can be fulfilled in the workplace: achievement, power, and affiliation.

Although most individuals will be influenced by all three of these motivators one may dominate an employee's specific work situation, depending on the employee and the circumstances:

- Employees who exhibit a strong need for achievement are likely to excel in work environments in which they can attain success largely on their own merits. Montana and Charnow refer to this as an entrepreneurial motivation.[3]

- Employees who are primarily motivated by power are likely to seek opportunities to lead and exert influence over others.

- Employees with a strong affiliation motivation will seek opportunities to work collaboratively with others.

The implications of McClelland's theories are two-fold[8]—one related to the individual and the other related to the task. For managers who recognize one of these three motivators as predominant in an employee, tasks should be selected or structured for that employee to allow him or her to engage in behaviors that are consistent with the characteristic motivator. Examples would be to choose tasks related to leadership for employees with a strong power motive, tasks related to group activities for employees with strong affiliation needs, and tasks associated with individual work for employees with high achievement needs. It may also be necessary to select tasks that will allow the employee to develop skills related to the other two motivators in order to help the employee "round out" or balance his or her skills appropriately.

When faced with a specific task that must be accomplished, managers should consider the relative strengths of these motivators when selecting an individual to accomplish the task. For autonomous, self-directed tasks, the manager may choose an individual with a strong achievement motive. For tasks that require coordination of a team of peers and co-workers, managers may choose individuals who have strong affiliation motives as team leaders. For tasks that require strong leadership and directive skills, managers may find that choosing an employee with high power motives may best accomplish the work.

In matching tasks and employees, it is important to consider development opportunities for the employees and the potential negative implications of unnecessarily "pigeon-holing" employees, thereby limiting their long-term development.

Action and Reward

B F Skinner[9] studied the impact of varying types of reinforcement on the behavior of employees. Behavior that was positively reinforced or rewarded, he theorized, was more likely to be repeated; behavior that was negatively reinforced or punished was less likely to be repeated. These concepts became known as behaviorism, operant conditioning, or reinforcement theory. These theories assume that the consequences of an employee's behavior determine future levels of performance. Taken to the extreme, these concepts may inappropriately reduce behaviors of employees into a series of stimuli (reinforcements) and responses (behaviors). For all but the most pessimistic observers of work behavior, humans are significantly more complex in their actions than behaviorism suggests. On the other hand, Victor Vroom[10] postulated that individuals do consider the likelihood of attaining personally preferred and desired outcomes as they choose their behaviors. Employees, then, actively contemplate and reflect on the results of any workplace behavior.

Vroom's Expectancy Theory suggests that organizations should clearly relate workplace rewards to employee performance. These rewards must be perceived by employees to be meaningful and desirable in order to be motivate them. Employees, the theory suggests, will actually calculate the likelihood that a given action on his or her part will lead to a desirable personal outcome. In order for the employee to pursue any given action, it is necessary that she or he realize the connection between that action and a possible reward. The greater the degree to which the employee believes that the reward is likely (the strength of the expectation of reward), the greater the strength of the motivation to complete the task.

References

1. Montana PJ, Charnow BH. *Management, 2nd Ed*. Haupauge, NY: Barrons; 1993.

2. Nosse LJ, Friberg DG, Kovacek PR. Managerial and Supervisory Principles for Physical Therapists. Baltimore, MD: Lippincott Williams and Wilkins; 1998.

3. Maslow AH. *Motivation and Personality*. New York, NY: Harper and Row; 1954.

4. Hersey P, Blanchard KH, Johnson DE. *Management of Organizational Behavior—Utilizing Human Resources, 7th Ed*. Upsaddle River, NJ: Prentice Hall; 1996.

5. Kovacek PR. Are physical therapists sliding down Maslow's hierarchy? *Advance for Physical Therapists and Physical Therapist Assistants*. Nov 9, 1998.

6. Herzberg F. *Work and the Nature of Man*. Cleveland, Ohio: World Publishing Company; 1966.

7. McGregor D. *The Human Side of Enterprise*. New York, NY: McGraw-Hill Book Co; 1960.

8. McClelland DC. *The Achieving Society*. Princeton, NJ: D Van Nostrand Company Inc; 1961.

9. Skinner BF. *Science and Human Behavior*. New York, NY: The Macmillan Company; 1953.

10. Vroom VH, Yetton P. *Leadership and Decision-Making*. Pittsburgh, Pa: University of Pittsburgh Press; 1973.

Chapter 8

Case Studies

Small Practice Case Study: Quality Physical Therapy Inc

Dale is very proud of his practice. Dale created Quality Physical Therapy Inc more than 6 years ago, and things are going well. Revenues are up. Dale's earnings as owner are above expectations. Staff morale is good. Patient/client care is living up to the name of the practice. Dale is finding that time is becoming more and more valuable and scarce. Staff size has grown to 15. Dale must now determine if it is time to create a new manager position within the practice.

Dale considers the decision to create an additional layer of management. There are several advantages for Dale and the practice if an additional manager works in the clinic. There are also some disadvantages. Dale decides to prepare a list of pros and cons to help him in making an informed decision (Table 1).

PROS	CONS
Dale will have more time for clinical care.	There will be costs associated with salary and benefits for the new manager.
Dale will have more time for marketing and networking.	Dale may become out of touch or removed from the daily operations of the practice.
Dale will be able to discuss strategy and human resource issues with the additional manager.	Dale will need to invest time to select and train the new manager.
There may be increased stability of the organization in the long run should anything happen to Dale in the future.	Staff may be confused by the chain of command.
Quality Physical Therapy Inc will be better positioned for future new sites.	Dale will have to learn to share decision-making authority.
Staff will have better access to management, if not directly to Dale.	Dale will need to decide specific authority and responsibilities for the new manager.

Table 1. *Pros and Cons for Adding a Management Layer at Quality Therapy Inc.*

Clearly this is a tough decision, but by identifying the potential obstacles to success, Dale can structure the new position in such a way that these obstacles are minimized.

Dale decides that the new management position should be pursued. At the next staff meeting, Dale asks the staff for input on this decision. Dale chooses to follow the communication pattern described by Tannenbaum and Schmidt[1] as a "tentative decision." Dale explains that hiring a new manager is tentatively the decision that has been made but that Dale wants staff input before proceeding. The staff members accept this process well and Dale prepares the following list of staff issues:

- Several staff members are concerned about access to Dale. Many have accepted jobs at Quality Physical Therapy Inc specifically because of the opportunity to work with Dale. These staff members feel that their quality of work life may be diminished if they are unable to interact with Dale on a regular basis.

- Several staff members express a desire to be included in the selection process for the new manager.

- After the staff meeting, several staff members indicate in private to Dale that they may be interested in applying for the new position.

- Several staff members share concerns about the loss of the feeling of family within the company. Any entrance of "outsiders," they feel, will reduce the closeness of the staff members and may have a negative impact on morale.

- Several staff members express concerns about the time and energy that will be required to "train" a new boss.

- Several staff members indicate that they do not see any benefits at all from this move, and they ask Dale to reconsider the decision to add a new manager.

As Dale mentally reviews the staff meeting, the situation becomes cloudy. To help clarify the situation, Dale reviews each of the staff comments in light of what is known about the motivation of persons in a work environment.

For the great majority of staff, Dale feels that they are acting in a manner consistent with what McGregor[2] termed Theory Y or what Ouchi[3] termed Theory Z. Dales sees the employees as having common goals and being both self-motivated and motivated to have the practice succeed.

For the staff members who are concerned about access to the owner, Dale recognizes the work of McClelland[4] related to employees who seek affiliation and the opportunity to work collaboratively with others. McClelland also discussed the motivation of employees to seek opportunities to lead and exert influence over others that is more likely when there is direct contact with the business owner.

Because a number of staff members have indicated a desire to be included in the selection process for the new manager, Dale reviews Herzberg's[5] writings on motivation and hygiene factors in the workplace. Dale feels that at least some of the staff members who want to have a say in the selection process are working to address the hygiene factors of administration and interpersonal relationships. Others may be seeking power—consistent again with McClelland's work. The staff members who have told Dale that they might be interested in applying for the new position may be seeking new challenges and the opportunity for personal and professional growth, consistent with many of the motivation theorists, including Maslow,[6] Herzberg,[5] and McClelland.[4]

The staff members who have shared concerns about the loss of the feeling of family within the company may be resistant to change or may be attempting to maintain a greater sense of basic security, based on Maslow's hierarchy.[6] This may also be true of the staff members who express concerns about the time and energy that will be required to "train" a new boss.

For the staff members who have indicated that they do not see any benefits at all from this move and who have asked Dale to reconsider the decision to add a new manager, Dale feels that change management theories[7] and Vroom's expectation theory[33] may best explain their behavior.

Given his improved understanding of the dynamics of the staff concerning this decision, Dale is much more comfortable proceeding with his plans to create a new managerial position.

Large Practice Case Study: St Margaret Hospital

TJ is the director of physical therapy at St Margaret Hospital, a large urban hospital. The physical therapy staff consists of the following:

- 15 physical therapists
- 6 physical therapist assistants
- 4 aides
- 3 clerical staff
- 1 director (80% administration, 20% patient care)
- 1 supervisor (50% patient care)

This staff provides services for inpatient medical/surgical patients at the hospital, residential rehabilitation in the 12-bed inpatient rehabilitation unit at the hospital, and outpatients at the hospital campus and one offsite satellite clinic.

The staff members are consistently excellent in providing high-quality clinical care. Many professional staff members are clinical specialists. The staff places a high priority on clinical continuing education.

Recently there have been serious cutbacks in reimbursement for physical therapy services for many types of services provided by TJ's department. Acute inpatient DRG rates have been dropping. The Medicare fee schedule for physical therapy services has resulted in much lower reimbursement than the cost reimbursement system that was in place prior to 1999. The inpatient rehabilitation unit is facing a change to a prospective payment system from the current cost reimbursement system that has been in place for many years. Discussions with the hospital finance department and APTA indicate that the trend to lower reimbursement rates for physical therapy is likely to continue in the future.

TJ is concerned that as reimbursement declines, contribution margins also will decline. The hospital administrator has asked TJ to prepare a plan to maintain or improve contribution margins for physical therapy services. This plan needs to be implemented very quickly.

At the next staff meeting, TJ discusses the situation with the staff and prepares a preliminary list of possible actions (Table 2) that would affect the contribution margin of the department. Each action is intended either to increase revenues or lower costs.

TJ reviews this list and feels that it is fairly complete, but he realizes that not all the actions listed are equally effective or desirable. TJ next prepares a list (Table 3) of all the possible actions and scores each according to its effectiveness and desirability. Note that the scores are the fictional subjective opinion of TJ only (ie, they are not meant to be suggestions by this author). In TJ's opinion, increasing productivity and merging with another department to share support services are likely to be the most effective actions, while improving charge capture and purchasing less-expensive supplies are, in his opinion, the most desirable choices (although he wonders if these latter two choices are really the most desirable or just the least undesirable choices identified).

Actions to Increase Revenue	Actions to Decrease Costs
■ Capture all charges for all services.	■ Purchase less-expensive or fewer supplies.
■ Increase individual and overall productivity.	■ Reduce payroll costs via salary freeze.
■ Raise prices.	■ Reduce payroll costs via hiring freeze.
■ Aggressively appeal all insurance rejections.	■ Reduce payroll costs via salary cut.
■ Review billing procedures for errors.	■ Reduce payroll costs by shifting to less-expensive employees.
■ Institute incentive program.	■ Cut management and non-clinical activities.
■ Aggressively market services to higher-reimbursement payers.	■ Merge departments with other similar areas of the hospital to share clerical and support staff.
	■ Reduce payroll by eliminating support personnel.

Table 2. *Possible Actions to Improve Contribution Margin at St Margaret Hospital Physical Therapy Department.*

Because the staff will be affected by any of these actions, TJ decides to ask for the staff's input in this process. At the next staff meeting, TJ distributes the "potential actions" list, without his scoring included, and asks the staff to individually score the table. The compiled results of this exercise are shown in Table 4.

Potential Actions	Effectiveness (1 high – 10 low)	Desirability (1 high – 10 low)
Actions to Increase Revenue		
Capture all charges for all services.	3	1
Increase individual and overall productivity.	1	3
Raise prices.	9	5
Aggressively appeal all insurance rejections.	6	4
Review billing procedures for errors.	4	2
Institute incentive program.	7	6
Aggressively market services to higher-reimbursement payers.	5	2
Actions to Decrease Costs		
Purchase less expensive or fewer supplies.	6	1
Reduce payroll costs via salary freeze.	4	8
Reduce payroll costs via hiring freeze.	3	4
Reduce payroll costs via salary cut.	2	10
Reduce payroll costs by shifting to less-expensive employees.	5	9
Cut management and non-clinical activities.	2	5
Merge departments with other similar areas of the hospital to share clerical and support staff.	1	3
Reduce payroll by eliminating support personnel.	7	7

Table 3. *Actions Scored by TJ Alone.*

In the staff's opinion, increasing productivity and a hiring freeze are likely to be the most effective actions. Instituting an incentive program and purchasing less expensive supplies are thought to be the most desirable choices.

The differences between TJ's scoring and that of the staff concern TJ. Because of the level of anxiety that the first two meetings with staff have caused, TJ decides not to directly involve the entire staff in the remainder of this process. TJ explains this position to the staff in an attempt to fully communicate and inform. Although several members of the staff continue to seek involvement in the decision process, there seems to be acceptance of TJ's decision to proceed without full staff input. Referring to the work of Tannenbaum and Schmidt,[1] TJ has started the decision process in the communication style of "present and decide" and is now moving to "present."

Potential Actions	Effectiveness (1 high – 10 low)	Desirability (1 high – 10 low)
Actions to Increase Revenue		
Capture all charges for all services.	4	6
Increase individual and overall productivity.	1	3
Raise prices.	9	2
Aggressively appeal all insurance rejections.	5	4
Review billing procedures for errors.	6	2
Institute incentive program.	2	1
Aggressively market services to higher-reimbursement payers.	5	3
Actions to Decrease Costs		
Purchase less-expensive or fewer supplies.	2	1
Reduce payroll costs via salary freeze.	8	8
Reduce payroll costs via hiring freeze.	1	3
Reduce payroll costs via salary cut.	7	10
Reduce payroll costs by shifting to less-expensive employees.	9	10
Cut management and non-clinical activities.	1	2
Merge departments with other similar areas of the hospital to share clerical and support staff.	6	5
Reduce payroll by eliminating support personnel.	5	9

Table 4. *Actions Scored by TJ's Staff.*

TJ reviews the success triad for the department: personnel, structure, and function. Clearly if there are to be changes in any of the three components, there will also have to be adjustments in the other two. If there were changes in the functions of the department, such as would be needed if departments merged or management and non-clinical activities were cut, there would have to be adjustments in personnel and structure. Changes in personnel, such as reducing support staff or shifting to less-expensive employees, would also require changes in functions and the structure of the department.

One of the most likely changes, in TJ's opinion, is to adjust the amount of management activity. This would allow more of TJ's and the supervisor's time for the clinical care of patients. Although TJ is aware that in many hospital departments, this can be a very effective step to increase productivity and revenue, he also acknowledges that in the physical therapy department at St Margaret Hospital, management overhead has already been reduced. TJ realizes that the management tasks still have to be done, whether or not there is an allotment of time to do them.

TJ reviews the management pyramid[9] and realizes that the department functions much like a freestanding organization in some ways. There are the three levels of management found in the pyramid: top management (TJ's boss), middle management (TJ as director), and supervisory management (supervisor). Removal of a layer of management may be a solution. However, even if there were not a supervisory management level in name, the functions would still have to be completed.

In reviewing the skills needed for functions at the supervisory management level, TJ realizes that those skills (technical skills, interpersonal skills, and conceptual skills) are needed in similar proportion for professional staff members. TJ decides to pursue involving the entire professional (therapist-level) staff in the management of the department. This would allow elimination of the supervisor position, at a minor cost saving. The most significant gains would be in the dissemination of supervisory management functions across all staff. TJ believes that would be very effective in helping the physical therapists understand the current health care environment, reimbursement policy, and departmental direction and would have a positive effect on productivity and department morale in the challenging times to come.

To help the physical therapist staff make the transition to more active involvement in department management, TJ distributes the APTA Section on Administration (now Health Policy and Administration) LAMP document[10] (see Appendix). This provides a strong starting point for the staff/managerial development activities that will be needed as the department positions itself for the future.

References

1. Tannebaum R, Schmidt WH. How to choose a leadership pattern. *Harvard Business Review*. May-June 1973.

2. McGregor D. *The Human Side of Enterprise*. New York, NY: McGraw-Hill Book Co; 1960.

3. Ouchi W. *Theory Z: How American Business Can Meet the Japanese Challenge*. Reading, Mass: Addison-Wesley; 1981.

4. McClelland DC. *The Achieving Society*. Princeton, NJ: D Van Nostrand Company Inc; 1961.

5. Herzberg F. *Work and the Nature of Man*. Cleveland, Ohio: World Publishing Company; 1966.

6. Maslow AH. *Motivation and Personality*. New York, NY: Harper and Row; 1954.

7. Kovacek PR. *Managing Employees in Changing Times*. Harper Woods, Mich: KMS; 1996.

8. Vroom VH, Yetton P. *Leadership and Decision-Making*. Pittsburgh, Pa: University of Pittsburgh Press; 1973.

9. Boone LE, Kurtz DL. *Contemporary Business, 7th Ed*. New York, NY: Dryden Press; 1993.

10. Section on Administration [now Section on Health Policy and Administration], American Physical Therapy Association. *Leadership, Administration, Management, and Professionalism*. Alexandria, Va: American Physical Therapy Association; 1998. Available at http://www.aptasoa.org. Accessed on December 16, 2002.

Glossary

Bureaucracy

Organizational structure involving governance by compartmentalization.

Business

An economic entity.

Competition

External organizations that offer similar or substitute products or services similar markets.

Contingency School

A theory of management that suggests that there is no universally acceptable explanation for all contemporary work related behaviors.

Delegation

Assigning work as a manager or supervisor that entrusts others with responsibility and authority and creates accountability for results.

Job Enrichment

The process of expanding a job's content to provide employees with increased opportunity to experience personal responsibility and meaning.

Job Enhancement

The process of adding more variety of tasks and duties to the job so that it is not as routine, mundane or repetitious.

Leadership

The aspect of management involving the influence of individuals towards the achievement of organizational or group goals.

Management by Objectives

Interactive process between manager and subordinate whereby they jointly identify and agree upon the subordinate's measurable work goals, define each of their responsibilities for achieving agreed upon goals, and use goal accomplishment as a guide for examining and evaluating the subordinate's performance.

Management Theory

The body of knowledge that attempts to understand how people behave in a work environment.

Management

The process of obtaining, deploying, and utilizing a variety of essential resources in support of an organization's objectives; working with and through other people to accomplish the objectives of both the organization and its members; the achievement of organizational objectives through people and other resources.

Matrix Organization

An organization in which some individuals report to two or more managers.

Mission Statement

A written document identifying why an organization exists.

Organization Chart

A graphical depiction of the reporting relationships in an organization.

Organizational Influence

The process of being in a position to effect change within an organization.

Organizational Development

A field of applied behavioral science focused on understanding and managing organizational change.

Quality of Work Life

Programs and processes in place to improve the overall quality of the work environment and the work itself.

Scientific Management

The systematic processes that include management principles and measurement to analyze tasks and activities that take place in a work environment in an effort to improve work output.

Span of Control

The number of employees who directly report to a manager or other person in a leadership position.

Supervision

The act of overseeing another's work.

Vision Statement

A simple, brief, inspirational, and public document intended to advance a futuristic view of an organization to its members and other stakeholders.

Appendix

LAMP Document
(excerpted with permission of the Section on Health Policy and Administration, accessible at www.aptasoa.org)

In 1998, a task force on leadership, administration, and management preparation was convened in response to a charge by the American Physical Therapy Association's Section on Administration (SOA) membership and Executive Committee. The result was the following document. The Section on Administration has since merged with the APTA Section on Health Policy, Legislation, and Regulation, now known as the Section on Health Policy and Administration.

Values/Beliefs Related to Leadership, Administration, Management, and Professionalism (LAMP)

One of the most important functions of leadership is to define those things that the group members collectively believe in. The following statements, we believe, are core beliefs that are critical to the adequate development of LAMP skills. They are divided into statements of beliefs about: LAMP skills themselves, educational strategies to facilitate LAMP skills, and educational resources required to facilitate LAMP skills.

Core Beliefs about LAMP Skills

- LAMP skills are required of all physical therapists, not just those with the title of manager.

- LAMP skills are necessary for the development of the effective professional.

- Business values promote the core values of physical therapists—they are not mutually exclusive.

- Physical therapists must be competent in the development and assessment of all types of outcomes, including both clinically related functional and business related operational outcomes.

- Understanding of the business environment is complementary to effective clinical decision-making.

- Clinical management is strongly influenced by the business environment.

- LAMP skills, in the context of a rapidly changing health care environment, can and often do have a significant impact on the influence of the profession—especially within large organizations.

- The quality of patient care and potential career advancement of clinicians, including employability, and long term practice and professional success will be compromised for those who do not incorporate the basic tenets of LAMP into their daily practice.

- Evaluation and assessment of self, peers, and systems is not unique to the role of the manager—it is a basic professional responsibility and a life skill.

- Basic generic abilities are essential components of the repertoire of behaviors essential for clinical success.[1]

- Commitment to learning, interpersonal skills, communication skills, effective use of time and resources, use of constructive feedback, problem solving, professionalism, responsibility, critical thinking, stress management.

Core Beliefs about Educational Strategies to Develop LAMP Skills

- No single learning format or structure is preferred to foster LAMP skill development.

- Student prior knowledge, skills and attitudes related to LAMP should be assessed and considered in the design of educational experiences.

- LAMP skills will be best developed when they are integrated throughout the educational experience and not only as a capstone course at the end of the curriculum.

- LAMP skills are built on a foundation of business ethics, law, organizational development and decision-making models.

- Educational process and content from other disciplines can be valuable when applied to Physical Therapy.

Core Beliefs about Educational Resources Needed to Develop LAMP Skills

- All members of the academic and clinical education faculty should value LAMP skills and seek ways to demonstrate this to students, patients and other health care professionals.

- Faculty development activities must include ongoing LAMP skills, however, no single career path uniquely qualifies faculty to foster student LAMP skill development.

- SOA must be a resource to its members and to others who are involved in the education of students in areas of LAMP.

- SOA, in conjunction with APTA and other components of APTA, should develop mechanisms to foster LAMP skills development in all physical therapists (clinicians, educators and researchers).

Content of the LAMP Process

Throughout the discussions of the task force, a consistent theme was the need to integrate the development of business related skills into the processes used to develop clinical skills. In order to encourage this process, the task force members examined the *Guide to Physical Therapist Practice* (Guide) and the *Normative Model of Physical Therapist Professional Education*. (It is noted that several of the task force members participated in activities that lead to the development of these two resources.)

The process that the Guide presents for clinical problem solving as the five elements of patient/client management[2] is very consistent with the problem solving activities related to LAMP skills. The figure below shows the conversion of Figure 2 in the Guide for business management rather than patient/client management. In essence, the five steps of examination, evaluation, diagnosis, prognosis, and intervention are unchanged. The specific content of each of the steps is different due to the nature of examining businesses or organizations rather than patients. The end result, hopefully, is optimal outcomes.

We believe that this model of business problem solving will facilitate the integration of clinical skills with business skills for physical therapists. We also welcome discussion of the model for suggestions and revisions to enhance its usefulness.

Within this revised problem-solving model, there are also specific content areas. The task force identified the following as examples of likely components of LAMP experiences.

Examination

Environmental scanning
- Historical perspective
- Profession
- Health care industry
- Business unit
- Public policy

Systems review
- Regulatory
- Reimbursement
- Legal
- Societal—national and global
- Political
- Economic (medical market basket)
- Demand management
- Disease management

Tests and measures
- Operational measures
  - Profit and loss analysis
  - Balance sheet analysis
  - Cash flow analysis
  - Receivables analysis
  - Accounts payable analysis
  - Budget/variance analysis
  - Ratio analysis
  - Cost analysis

Evaluation

Operational business analysis
- Interpretation of findings in tests and measures
- Business success measures
  - Quality
  - Quantity
  - Reimbursement
  - Cost containment measures
  - Satisfaction measures
  - Clinical and functional outcomes
  - Human resource measures
  - External accreditation agencies

Diagnosis

Strategic analysis
Gap analysis of current business condition to target condition

Prognosis

Long-term planning
Interpretation of current conditions in context of business health

Intervention

Operations

Core content:
  Budgeting
  Marketing (products and services)
  Professional/business ethics
  Facility planning
  Personnel management
  Diversity
  Conflict
  Stress management
  Time management
  Staff counseling
  Staff mentoring
  Staff development

Management information systems/data systems/telehealth
Reimbursement/risk assessment
Documentation
Quality assessment/quality improvement/utilization review/peer review
Continuous quality improvement

Direct service delivery
  Coordination
  Communication
  Instruction
  Documentation
  Contracting
Negotiating
Outsourcing
Networking
Systems analysis (organizational systems)
International management
Organizational change systems
Cost management

Outcomes

Compare condition to objective
Compare condition in environmental scanning in context of current operations
Return to systems review
Environmental scanning is a continuous process

The task force also identified several content areas that will typically be examined in greater detail. This list is not exhaustive but rather is offered as a starting point for further discussions.

Leadership

Mentorship
Role models
Communication
Listening skills
Risk taking
Motivation
Visioning
Organizational influence
Change facilitation/management
Networking skills
Professional involvement

Management

Organizational and management theory
Policy and procedure development
Job descriptions
Organizational development
Facility management
Daily operations
Project management
Personnel management

Performance planning and appraisal
Staff recruitment and retention
Motivation
Career ladders
Discipline, coaching, and counseling
Meeting efficiency
Professional personnel development
Delegation/supervision
Strategic planning and management
Job search skills (employment process)
Effective use of all resources
Managing across the continuum
Structure, restructuring, and re-engineering
Interdisciplinary and transdisciplinary management
Team building
Continuous organizational improvement
Challenges of managing the knowledge worker

References

1.   May W, Morgan B, Lemke J, Karst G, Stone H. Model for ability-based assessment in physical therapist education. *Journal of Physical Therapy Education.* 1995;9(1):3-6.)

2.   Guide to physical therapist practice, 2nd ed. *Phys Ther.* 2001;81:9-744.

Final Examination

To receive continuing education units for this course, please answer the following multiple-choice questions and return this completed answer sheet *and* the Evaluation Questionnaire to APTA either by e-mail to ceutests@apta.org, by fax to 703/706-3387, or by mail to APTA, 1111 North Fairfax Street, Alexandria, VA 22314.

Your Certificate of Completion and CEU Award will be sent to you upon receipt and successful completion of your final examination.

Coming in 2008! Complete the final exam and print your CEU certificate online. Access the APTA Learning Center from the convenience of your home or office. Check www.apta.org for updates.

There is only one BEST answer. Successful completion of this test is a score of 70% or higher.

1. Strategic planning involves all of the following concepts, *except*:
    a) Making all business decisions to maximize profits.
    b) Making decisions in a risky environment.
    c) Using a systematic approach to making decisions.
    d) Involving all necessary stakeholders in the process.

2. The element of strategic planning that represents the greatest difficulty is:
    a) Spending a large sum of money.
    b) Bringing together an uncooperative staff.
    c) Identifying ways to make objectives measurable.
    d) Understanding and predicting the future.

3. According to Drucker, which of the following is the most critical question   managers should ask themselves to define their businesses?
    a) What level of profit do we want to make?
    b) Who is the customer?
    c) How much space and equipment do we need to do our work?
    d) What kind of personnel mix do we need to meet our objectives?

4. The best time to engage in strategic planning is:
    a) When the business is in crisis.
    b) When a supervisor requires it.
    c) Continually.
    d) When a new manager is employed.

5. Collins and Porras identify using BHAGs as a way to help produce an envisioned future. BHAGs are:
   a) Brave, humongous, ape-like giants.
   b) Big, hairy, audacious goals.
   c) Big, highly organized, autonomous goals.
   d) Bryan's human assessment games.

6. The Delbecq technique is especially useful to overcome all of the following except:
   a) One group member who volunteers much more than the others.
   b) The need to obtain opinions from international experts.
   c) One group member who never participates in the group activities.
   d) A group that frequently becomes very argumentative.

7. SWOT analysis includes the following attributes of a business:
   a) Strengths, weaknesses, opportunities, and threats.
   b) Stipends, worth analysis, organizational dynamics, and time motion analysis.
   c) Speech pathologists, weight training specialists, and occupational therapists.
   d) Successful work oriented teams.

8. One of the differences between CPM and PERT is that:
   a) PERT identifies the minimum time needed to accomplish the task.
   b) CPM, but not PERT, identifies the specific activities needed to complete the task.
   c) CPM identifies the minimum time needed to accomplish the entire project.
   d) A PERT diagram includes a calendar of events.

9. A deontologic approach to ethical decision making is based on:
   a) The environment in which the potential action will occur.
   b) The potential affect of the action on all stakeholders.
   c) The desire to be as kind as possible.
   d) The rules that are assumed to be absolute in a particular society.

10. A teleologic approach to ethical decision making is based on:
    a) The environment in which the potential action will occur.
    b) The potential affect of the action on all stakeholders.
    c) The desire to be as kind as possible.
    d) The rules that are assumed to be absolute in a particular society.

11. The American Physical Therapy Association has many documents that can assist in strategic planning and ethical decision-making. Identify the one document in this list that will be least useful for this purpose.
    a) *Guide to Physical Therapist Practice*
    b) *Code of Ethics*
    c) *Standards of Practice for Physical Therapy*
    d) *Writing Case Reports*

12. Which of the following are definitions of management?
    a) The process of obtaining, deploying and utilizing a variety of essential resources in support of an organization's objectives
    b) Working with and through other people to accomplish the objectives of both the organization and its members
    c) The process of getting things done through people
    d) All of the above

13. True or False: In order to be effective in the clinical care of patients, every physical therapist must be competent in the business aspects of our profession.
    a) True
    b) False

14. True or False: Only a physical therapist should manage the business of a physical therapy service or practice.
    a) True
    b) False

15. The three layers of the management pyramid are:
    a) Executive, legislative, judicial.
    b) Top, middle, lower.
    c) Executive, department, supervisory.
    d) Top, middle, supervisory.

16. The three components of the success triad are:
    a) People, facilities, environment.
    b) Personnel, structure, function.
    c) Managers, employees, buildings.
    d) Managers, employees, environment.

17. Top management requires the greatest emphasis on:
    a) Technical skills.
    b) Interpersonal skills.
    c) Conceptual skills.
    d) Negotiation skills.

18. The factors of change in order of difficulty to change (from least to most difficult) are:
    a) Knowledge, attitudes, individual behavior and group behavior.
    b) Attitude, group behavior and physical plant.
    c) Knowledge, motivation, self actualization and behavior.
    d) Attitudes, morale, individual behavior and group behavior.

19. The four stages of change acceptance, in order, are:
    a) Denial, resistance, attitude, commitment.
    b) Denial, refusal, new awareness, commitment.
    c) Denial, resistance, new awareness, acceptance.
    d) Denial, resistance, new awareness, commitment.

20. What are the Elements of Clinical and Business Management Leading to Optimal Outcomes according to the APTA Section on Administration's Position on Leadership, Administration and Management Processes?
    a) Examination, treatment, documentation and follow up
    b) Examination, evaluation, diagnosis, prognosis, intervention and outcomes
    c) Evaluation, intervention, outcomes
    d) Knowledge, attitudes, documentation, intervention and follow-up

21. The success planning cycle consists of which of the following steps?
    a) Mission statement, goal setting, task identification, accountability, evaluation
    b) Examination, evaluation, diagnosis, prognosis, intervention, outcomes
    c) Vision, mission, objectives, tasks, time lines, follow up
    d) Vision, goals, tasks, accountabilities, follow up

22. Who is the father of scientific management?
    a) Abraham Maslow
    b) Frederick Herzberg
    c) Frederick Taylor
    d) Frank Gilbreth

23. Mayo's Hawthorne experiments demonstrated:
    a) The need to consider lighting in facility design.
    b) The need to consider human aspects of work performance.
    c) The need to rank human motivations in order to understand work performance.
    d) The need to recognize the difference between factors of motivation and factors of hygiene to understand work performance.

24. Herzberg's theories of motivation demonstrated:
    a) The need to consider lighting in facility design.
    b) The need to consider human aspects of work performance.
    c) The need to rank human motivations in order to understand work performance.
    d) The need to recognize the difference between factors of motivation and factors of hygiene to understand work performance.

25. Maslow's theories emphasized:
    a) The need to consider lighting in facility design.
    b) The need to consider human aspects of work performance.
    c) The need to rank human motivations in order to understand work performance.
    d) The need to recognize the difference between factors of motivation and factors of hygiene to understand work performance.

Business Skills in Physical Therapy: Defining Your Business

Final Examination Answer Sheet

Please print or type.

Identification number: _____

Name: _____

Social Security number (optional): _____

Mailing address: _____

City/state/zip: _____

Daytime phone: _____

It is very important that you include your daytime phone number is case there are any questions that we have about your final examination.

Course title: Business Skills in Physical Therapy: Defining Your Business

---

Instructions:

Circle your response ◯.

To change your response, cross out the incorrect response ⊗ and circle the correct response ◯.

1.	a	b	c	d	14.	a	b		
2.	a	b	c	d	15.	a	b	c	d
3.	a	b	c	d	16.	a	b	c	d
4.	a	b	c	d	17.	a	b	c	d
5.	a	b	c	d	18.	a	b	c	d
6.	a	b	c	d	19.	a	b	c	d
7.	a	b	c	d	20.	a	b	c	d
8.	a	b	c	d	21.	a	b	c	d
9.	a	b	c	d	22.	a	b	c	d
10.	a	b	c	d	23.	a	b	c	d
11.	a	b	c	d	24.	a	b	c	d
12.	a	b	c	d	25.	a	b	c	d
13.	a	b							

Please return this completed answer sheet *and* the Evaluation Questionnaire to APTA either by e-mail to ceutests@apta.org, by fax to 703/706-3387, or by mail to APTA, 1111 North Fairfax Street, Alexandria, VA 22314.

Your Certificate of Completion and CEU Award will be sent to you within 4 weeks upon receipt and successful completion of your final examination.

Coming in 2008! Complete the final exam and print your CEU certificate online. Access the APTA Learning Center from the convenience of your home or office. Check www.apta.org for updates.

Business Skills in Physical Therapy: Defining Your Business

Evaluation Questionnaire
Please help APTA serve your continuing education needs more effectively by taking a few minutes to complete this evaluation, and returning, along with your Final Examination Answer Sheet, to APTA either by e-mail to ceutests@ apta.org or by fax to 703/706-3387. We look forward to your response!

Course Evaluation

	Strongly Disagree	Disagree	Neither Agree nor Disagree	Agree	Strongly Agree
Content matched **written** description	☐	☐	☐	☐	☐
Content is **applicable** to practice	☐	☐	☐	☐	☐
Method of delivery was **useful**	☐	☐	☐	☐	☐
Examination questions **reflected** content	☐	☐	☐	☐	☐
Course level was **appropriate**	☐	☐	☐	☐	☐
Course met my **needs**	☐	☐	☐	☐	☐

Rate the quality of this course:
☐ Well below expectations ☐ Below expectations ☐ Met Expectations ☐ Above Expectations
☐ Well Above Expectations

If you checked "Well below expectations" or "Below expectations" above, please indicate why:
_____
_____
_____

How much time did it take to complete this course? _____

How did you find out about this course?
☐ *PT Magazine* advertisement
☐ APTA Web site
☐ APTA Resource Catalog
☐ Word of mouth
☐ Other _____

I selected this course because of the (check all that apply):
☐ Content
☐ Course author
☐ Opportunity to study at home
☐ Cost
☐ Other _____

Topics in which I am most interested in gaining new knowledge are:

Topic 1 _____
Topic 2 _____

Learner Demographics

I am an APTA member: ☐ Yes ☐ No

I am a: ☐ PT ☐ PTA

How many years?
☐ 1-5
☐ 6-10
☐ 11-15
☐ 16-20
☐ 21-25
☐ Over 25

Type of facility in which you practice most often:
☐ Acute care hospital
☐ Health and wellness facility
☐ Health system or hospital based on outpatient facility or clinic
☐ Industry
☐ Patient's home/home care
☐ Post secondary
☐ Private outpatient office or group practice
☐ Research center
☐ School system (preschool/primary/secondary)
☐ SNF/ECF/ICE
☐ Sub-acute rehab hospital (inpatient)
☐ Other _____

I am most involved/interested in the following areas of practice (Check all that apply)

☐ Acute Care/Hospital Clinical
☐ Administration
☐ Aquatic Physical Therapy
☐ Cardiopulmonary
☐ Clinical Electrophysiology
☐ Education
☐ Geriatrics
☐ Hand Rehabilitation
☐ Health Policy, Legislation, Regulation
☐ Home Health

☐ Neurology
☐ Oncology
☐ Orthopedics
☐ Pediatrics
☐ Private Practice
☐ Research
☐ Sports Physical Therapy
☐ Veterans Affairs
☐ Women's Health

Here is an "open line" to APTA! Please let us know how we can improve our services:

_____
_____
_____
_____
_____

Notes

Notes